Cecilia M. Espinosa • Laura Ascenzi-Moreno

Foreword by Ofelia Ga

Rooted in STRENGTH

Using Translanguaging to Grow Multilingual Readers and Writers

SCHOLASTIC

A mi Padre que sé que
a sus 89 años se levanta cada día
como si fuera su primer día.
—*Cecilia*

To Matteo and Marco, who expand
my humanity every day.
—*Laura*

Publisher/content editor: Lois Bridges
Editorial director: Sarah Longhi
Editor-in-chief: Raymond Coutu
Senior editor: Shelley Griffin
Production editor: Danny Miller
Designer: Maria Lilja

Photos ©: cover boy: shisu_ka/Shutterstock; cover girl: Jose Girarte/Getty Images; 17: SDI Productions/Getty Images; 41: wavebreakmedia/Shutterstock; 73: Catcher of Light, Inc./Shutterstock; 78: Scholastic Inc.; 95: kali9/Getty Images; 110: kali9/Getty Images; 137: KidStock/Getty Images; icons throughout: The Noun Project and RedKoala/Shutterstock. All other photos courtesy of Dr. Cecilia M. Espinosa and Dr. Laura Ascenzi-Moreno.

Excerpt from *Guacamole: Un poema para cocinar / A Cooking Poem* by Jorge Argueta copyright © 2012 by Jorge Argueta. Reprinted by permission of Groundwood Books. "Differentiated Miscue Analysis Form" from the article "Translanguaging and Responsive Assessment Adaptations: Emergent Bilingual Readers" by Laura Ascenzi-Moreno from *Language Arts*, Vol. 95, No. 6, July 2018. Copyright © 2018 by the National Council of Teachers of English. Reprinted with permission. Excerpt from *Soñadores / Dreamers* by Yuyi Morales copyright © 2018 by Yuyi Morales, translation copyright © 2018 by Yuyi Morales. Reprinted by permission of Holiday House Publishing, Inc. All rights reserved.

CONTENTS

ACKNOWLEDGMENTS

It turns out that writing a book—just like teaching—is about being rooted in communities. We are so grateful for the many circles that nurture, sustain, and propel us into new adventures.

We would like to thank our CUNY NYSIEB familia, our leaders—Ofelia García, Ricardo Otheguy, Kate Menken, and each director and member of this project. Thank you for inviting us to engage in a transformative paradigm shift about bilingualism. Thank you, Ofelia, for saying, "I see a book in these ideas," after we wrote "A Translanguaging Pedagogy for Writing: A CUNY-NYSIEB Guide for Educators."

No book project is ever possible without a team of editors and others who work so seamlessly together. We thank Lois Bridges, Ray Coutu, Sarah Longhi, Danny Miller, and Maria Lilja.

The seeds for my ideas (Cecilia) about what it meant to become a teacher of emergent bilinguals were planted on the first day I joined the vibrant community at Machan School. Here I learned to take a perspective of strength, as we looked closely at children and their work. I am grateful for my lifelong mentors, Sarah Hudelson and Karen Smith.

At Lehman College/CUNY, my experiences are enriched daily by our students, as well as all my colleagues in the ECCE Department, the Lehman Library, The New York City Writing Project, and Writing Across the Curriculum. To the many teachers from whom I have learned, gracias por mantenerme conectada a la tierra y llena de esperanza.

Gracias, Laura, por tu sabiduría and for making this journey of writing this book together such a joy. Finally, to my family in the U.S. and Ecuador for always being ready for a hike. And to Emilia, Lucas, Julian, and Isabel for ensuring that bilingualism IS the norm.

I am grateful for the educators at the Cypress Hills Community School, where I (Laura) was a dual-language bilingual teacher and coach for over a decade. Many thanks to my supportive, caring, and brave administrators at the Brooklyn College School of Education and to the kind, critical, and engaged faculty in the Childhood, Bilingual, and Special Education Department. My Brooklyn College students are my heart—they inspire me and push me—endless thank yous to former and future students. I also want to thank the members of the PiLaCS research team.

Mil gracias a Cecilia, a kindred spirit, who lifts up the power of listening to the child as the starting point of all teaching and learning. I thank my mother who cradled me in stories of Boyacá, Colombia, which made me a literate person from day one. And none of this would have been possible without my husband, Gian Luca, and children, Matteo and Marco, for filling my life with crazy and loving days.

FOREWORD

Seeing Over the Translanguaging Corriente and Into Classrooms

Ofelia García, The Graduate Center, City University of New York

How do we ensure that the translanguaging corriente that flows through the lives and languaging of multilingual children neither stagnates nor flows out of classrooms? How can teachers ensure that the translanguaging corriente moves their classroom teaching and their students' learning? Espinosa and Ascenzi-Moreno find the answers by rooting translanguaging in the strength, resolve, and resourcefulness of the emergent bilinguals that we see clearly in this book. By focusing on the actions of the students around reading and writing propelled by teachers who leverage the children's translanguaging, the authors bring forth the strengths of emergent bilinguals as they interact with texts.

This is a book that brings into sharp relief the act of seeing emergent bilinguals deeply. The precise and careful language with which Espinosa and Ascenzi-Moreno describe these experiences enables readers to actually see translanguaging at work in the literacy education of emergent bilingual children. The gift of this book to teachers is that it opens up their vision, allowing them to visualize the possibilities and to feel the potential before being asked to understand a theory. Rather than dwelling on developing teachers' understandings and knowledge of translanguaging, this book focuses on vision: "What does translanguaging into literacy by emergent bilingual children look like in classrooms?"

Ofelia García is Professor Emerita in the Ph.D. programs in Urban Education and Latin American, Iberian and Latino Cultures at The Graduate Center of the City University of New York. The American Educational Research Association has awarded her three Lifetime Research Achievement Awards—Distinguished Contributions to Social Contexts in Education (2019), Bilingual Education (2017), and Second Language Acquisition Leadership through Research (2019). She is a member of the U.S. National Academy of Education. For more, visit www.ofeliagarcia.org.

Teachers often find the concept of translanguaging too fluid, too slippery. They may understand it, but in the act of teaching, they find que se les va de las manos, as it slips out of their hands and classrooms when pressed to react to external bureaucratic demands. Scripted curricula, pacing calendars, and classroom textbooks aligned to meaningless language standards all squeeze the life out of the translanguaging corriente in the classroom. But now, Espinosa and Ascenzi-Moreno throw teachers a lifeline to help them ensure that the corriente is a vibrant resource in the classroom. The rootedness of the current has nothing to do with external conditions, with boundaries, with state regulations, with education tradition; it has to do with children themselves, with their strengths, and with their creative and imaginative individualities. The classroom is not simply a ship anchored in a translanguaging current. The classroom is children, all rooted in their own strengths as the translanguaging corriente is allowed to flow.

By rooting the work in the children's strengths, the authors enable teachers "to see" over the translanguaging corriente and into classrooms. This expanded vision is accomplished by describing teachers' actions over boundaries imposed by named languages, named subjects, named pedagogies, and focusing instead on the students themselves and their lives in classrooms.

The authors take us over boundaries of languages, literacy components, and pedagogical practices, and provide teachers with explicit guidance. Additionally, since the authors focus on children's strengths through the teachers' actions they describe, these processes are presented holistically. We "see" the reading process—shared reading, guided reading, read-alouds, independent reading, author and literature studies—from the perspective of those who are experiencing it, children and teachers. We "see" the writing process and the different possibilities—language experience approach, interactive writing, shared writing, writing conferences, publications, and writing celebrations—through the teachers' and the children's eyes. That is why there is no need to talk specifically about biliteracy, since for the teachers and the bilingual children who appear in this book, every literacy act is bilingual and biliterate. Whether the teachers are focusing on reading or writing, emergent bilingual children are portrayed in this book listening, speaking, role-playing, drawing, writing graffiti, engaging in visual essays, and even coding. And they are pictured translanguaging, using their full repertoire even when the text they are listening to, reading, writing, or performing has been rendered by its creator in one language and one mode. The literacy processes in which these emergent bilingual children engage are always multilingual and multimodal.

There is a wealth of resources contained in this book, including children's literature titles. However, the literature resources do not appear as simple lists. The books are always being used by teachers and students. The texts, just as the language of the texts, are not considered self-contained. Rather, the texts and their assigned language extend beyond the actual pages, bringing into focus the children's actions with their entire linguistic and semiotic repertoires, the complexity and intertwining of their lives—together with those of their families and communities.

To describe translanguaging and literacy in ways that are rooted in the strengths of emergent bilingual children requires sophisticated understandings of theory. It requires theory to be not only understood in the head, but also, felt in the gut and performed in the body. Espinosa and Ascenzi-Moreno engage the readers not just in thinking about translanguaging and literacy, but in envisioning it in the classroom, feeling what it provides, and performing it with their actions.

Regarding the assessment of reading and writing, the authors write, "Many educators believe assessment should be data-driven, but we believe it should always be student-driven" (p. 207). Both chapters on Assessments in the book are titled "Seeing the Emergent Bilingual Reader/Writer." This is in essence what this book does. It is student-driven and propelled by the emergent bilingual readers/writers' strengths. And it reminds us that all acts of teaching and assessing are acts of seeing, viewing the emergent bilinguals from the inside-out, with their translanguaging potential. The book provides us with ways of rooting our vision in the strength of emergent bilingual students, enabling teachers to feel the translanguaging corriente and to steer it in ways that grow multilingual readers and writers.

Rooted in Strength

"Unless we begin to understand what our students know, how they know it, and what they value about it, we waste their time. Worse, if our students think we don't know something special about them, which they value, they may find learning to be an isolated and meaningless exercise."

—DONALD H. GRAVES

For a teacher, one of the greatest pleasures is to see students deeply engaged in using reading and writing as tools for thinking, expressing, wondering, and knowing. When we were new teachers, we looked for strategies to engage our emergent bilinguals—students who use two or more languages in their daily lives—in rich, thoughtful literacy practices. After years of working as bilingual teachers and university professors, we concluded that in order to assist emergent bilinguals in their journeys to becoming confident and capable learners with strong identities as readers and writers, instructional strategies cannot stand alone. Rather, all pedagogy needs to be rooted in the fact that emergent bilinguals' full participation as readers and writers is fundamental to any classroom where all students deeply engage in literacy.

Who Is This Book For?

- All teachers who count emergent bilinguals as part of their classroom communities.
- Classroom teachers who have one or two emergent bilingual students.
- Teachers of English as a new language (ENL).
- Bilingual teachers who practice in a variety of bilingual programs: early late-exit programs or dual-language bilingual (DLB) programs.
- Teachers who are looking for new ways to work with their emergent bilinguals.
- Teachers who are just starting their journeys to becoming thoughtful and skillful educators of emergent bilinguals.

In this book, we advocate for and offer a vision of the education of emergent bilinguals. We explain practical ways in which they can fully engage in literacy by using their entire linguistic and sociocultural repertoires. We show you how you can support your emergent bilinguals in becoming readers and writers not only through what you specifically *do* for them, but also in how you *think* about them and how they learn through and about language. Our goal is to help you understand and connect to robust views of how emergent bilinguals learn language and literacy. We'll introduce you to tools for transforming your reading and writing instruction, while supporting emergent bilinguals through leveraging the resources they bring to school—thus rooting instruction in students' strengths.

What Kind of Bilingual Education Programs Are There?

What all bilingual programs have in common is that they use two named languages in instruction, for example, Spanish and English. A late-exit bilingual program refers to one in which emergent bilingual students are instructed in two languages but ultimately transition to a monolingual English program. This is in contrast to a dual-language bilingual program in which the goal is for students to become bilingual and bicultural. Typically, late-exit bilingual programs have targeted language-minoritized students, while dual-language bilingual programs include both language-minoritized students and monolingual English speakers.

We hope that teachers across a spectrum of experiences—from those who are just getting started to those who have taught for decades—will find innovative ideas that help them create classrooms that support emergent bilinguals' literacy. As former early childhood and elementary school teachers and now teacher educators, we primarily support teachers from kindergarten through fifth grade, knowing that teachers who work with other grade levels can easily adapt our principles.

Bringing a Bilingual Vision to Reading and Writing Instruction

As teachers, we loved reading professional books about the teaching of reading and writing. These books energized and inspired us, and they challenged us to envision the literacy classroom as a space where children have a voice in a vibrant and diverse community of readers and writers.

But when we returned to our classrooms to implement what we had learned, we encountered a big challenge. Too many of the books that we found so inspiring assumed that English was the standard bearer of meaning-making in the classroom. Many of our students, however, were bilingual and learning to read and write in English and Spanish. We needed to work on how to make reading and writing instruction fulfilling, exciting, and full of joy for our emergent bilinguals—even as they deepened their capacities to language.

Far too often, emergent bilinguals are asked to wait until their English is good enough to fully engage in the transformative vision for reading and writing that we aim to provide for all students. Or, they are asked to leave key aspects of their language repertoire at the classroom door. Emergent bilinguals' language differences, cultural resources, and educational histories are often seen as challenges, rather than as assets in their learning. We realized that we needed to figure out ways to consistently and deeply intertwine those assets with literacy learning.

Emergent bilinguals' language differences, cultural resources, and educational histories are often seen as challenges, rather than as assets in their learning.

As we looked back on the pivotal books that made a difference in our teaching, we realized that the common thread among them is an unwavering belief in the power of children to participate fully as readers and writers in their classrooms. All the professional authors who guided us portrayed children as strong, full of resources, and eager to learn to read and write. For them, the role of the teacher was to unleash, not mute, the powers that all children bring to school. While this view of children as resourceful, powerful language learners is echoed in current views of bilingualism, there are just a few professional books that advocate and outline how emergent bilinguals can participate fully in these types of literacy experiences in classrooms.

In this book, we look across research and teaching communities to create an understanding of literacy that incorporates strength-based multilingual approaches. We provide a layered perspective to base your teaching practices in students' strengths.

A Dynamic View of Bilingualism: Translanguaging

Translanguaging is a new way of thinking about language and the language practices of emergent bilinguals that is critical to designing effective and equitable instruction (García & Sánchez, 2018). Although translanguaging is often described as a language practice—when bilinguals use two or more languages to communicate—translanguaging encompasses much more. García & Li Wei (2014) characterize translanguaging as a *process* that weaves together people's linguistic and socio-historical resources to create new communicative practices. Li Wei writes (2011, p. 1223) that translanguaging

Translanguaging is a creative and critical process in which multilingual people use their language and other resources in dynamic, flexible, multimodal, semiotic, and purposeful ways.

"creates a social space for multilinguals . . . by bringing together different dimensions of their personal histories, experiences, and environments; their attitudes, beliefs, and ideologies; and their cognitive and physical capacities into one coordinated and meaningful performance." In other words, translanguaging is a creative and critical process in which multilingual people use their language and other resources in dynamic, flexible, multimodal, semiotic, and purposeful ways. Translanguaging starts with the child and is shaped by the ways in which he or she interacts with and makes meaning of texts.

This is a radical departure from the traditional response to emergent bilinguals, who too often are actively discouraged from using all of their language resources in school, including any language other than English, because their teachers feel the best way to learn either content or language is without "interference" from another language. Emergent bilinguals are also often measured against their monolingual peers. For example, young children bring their knowledge of animal sounds based on what they've learned at home. At school, the teacher may only recognize the animal sounds as represented in English (e.g., a dog's bark is *woof woof* in English; however, in Spanish, it is *guau guau*). When educators view the differences as deficiencies, they miss out on enriching the classroom's linguistic repertoire. By "linguistic repertoire," we mean all the features of students' language practices that cut across named languages, like Spanish, Mandarin, and Arabic, and linguistic varieties within a specific named language. It is important to note that when students' language practices are emerging, they blend, combine, and create new uses with the language resources they have. With a translanguaging stance and approach, the starting point is how to build from the resources that emergent bilinguals bring to classrooms.

In this book, we offer ways to think about translanguaging and how it relates to the teaching of literacy and biliteracy—the "ability to bring the whole self and the entire language repertoire into the reading performance, regardless of the language of the text" (García, 2020, p. 558). Instead of providing you with strategies to tack onto a core reading and writing program, our aim is to help you re-envision reading and writing for emergent bilinguals where multilingualism is the norm and where emergent bilinguals are viewed as capable and full of resources that are essential to their literacy learning.

A student demonstrates how translanguaging is a way to express herself seamlessly.

Who Are Emergent Bilinguals?

We refer to students who use two or more named languages in their daily lives as emergent bilinguals. When García, Kleifgen, and Falchi first introduced the term in 2008, they were responding to a national trend to erase the word *bilingual* from the face of federal and state agencies. Terms such as *English Learner* and *Limited English Proficient* were used instead, emphasizing students' lack of English. Even a term such as *dual-language learners*, which refers to students by a type of bilingual program, erases students' bilingualism and bilingual identities. We strongly believe that the reference point for students should not be the type of program they are in. Therefore, we advocate that educators adopt strength-based terms such as *emergent bilingual* or *multilingual learner*. You may be thinking, "Here it comes again, a new term but nothing changes," but terms do matter because they shape our thinking about the capacity and potential of students and how we educate them. Labels for students also shape our policies, programs, and instruction (Brooks, 2020).

Emergent bilinguals have strengths that are unrecognized or under-recognized because they are measured against their monolingual peers. When emergent bilinguals are compared to monolinguals, what they lack tends to be highlighted, and not what they create and develop based on their experiences (García, personal communication, 3/20). We instead stress the word *emergent* in this term because it is the *emergence*, *recognition*, and *sustainability* of new equitable and meaningful literacy practices that emergent bilinguals bring to the classroom that hold potential for transforming literacy instruction. For that reason, it is critical that we move beyond using the term *emergent bilinguals* to refer solely to "English Language Learners," and instead use *emergent bilinguals* to challenge us as educators to recognize, harness, and build on students' strengths.

Emergent Bilinguals Are a Diverse Group

Emergent bilinguals represent a range of culturally and linguistically diverse students who were either born in the United States or who immigrated to the U.S. at different times of their lives. There are many children in the U.S. who are growing up bilingual. For those students, their home language is their entire linguistic repertoire. When we refer to linguistic repertoire we mean all features of students' language practices that cut across named languages, such as Spanish, Mandarin, Tagalog, Arabic, etc. While the term *home language* is appropriate for students who grow up monolingually either in the U.S. or another country, for students who grow up bilingually, their entire linguistic repertoire is their bilingualism. As teacher educators, we must keep this diversity in mind rather than simply categorizing children.

A Word on Linguistic Diversity

Although this book is geared to teachers who work with emergent bilinguals, it is also geared to teachers whose students speak different varieties of English. One language may have distinctive features, such as the ways words sound, different words for the same thing, or even different ways that language works. In the United States, for example, we have Black Vernacular English, New York City English (*Newyorkese*), and Chicano English. All language varieties are equal in terms of richness and complexity, although socially some are viewed more favorably than others. For students who speak in ways that are not typically valued in school and society, translanguaging pedagogy can be a useful and important tool.

For students who speak in ways that are not typically valued in school and society, translanguaging pedagogy can be a useful and important tool.

How This Book Is Organized

We want you, the reader, to take a journey with us. We have organized the book into three parts.

- **PART I: Translanguaging Into Literacy** We introduce the connections between literacy and translanguaging and explore the diversity among students and how our instructional environment, pedagogical stance, and techniques need to match that diversity.

- **PART II: Reading Into Meaning** We focus on the teaching of reading. We provide a short overview of reading research for emergent bilinguals and then explore how to apply translanguaging pedagogy to grow readers and writers. We also present ways to use formative reading assessments to understand how to support emergent bilinguals' development as readers.

- **PART III: Writing Into Understanding** We zero in on writing. We offer a summary of the research on writing instruction for emergent bilinguals. Then we address how to set the tone during writing time, the importance of using rich mentor texts, and the introduction of translanguaging writing tools. We end with guidance on conducting conferences with emergent bilingual students and asset-based writing assessments.

Features You Will Find

We hope you will find new ideas, inspiration, and ultimately the confidence to address the needs of emergent bilingual students and place them at the center of your instruction. Throughout the book we include recurring features to help you navigate each part.

Into the Classroom

In these vignettes, we illustrate how the ideas that we introduce in each chapter might look and feel in a classroom.

Actions

Inspired by Donald Graves, these short activities are meant to challenge you to explore concepts by applying them to your own teaching and learning experiences. They will jump-start personal reflection about your classroom and provide opportunities to connect with ideas in this book.
You can do them alone or with colleagues.

Suggestions for Professional Development

These are meant to propel you and your colleagues to discover how translanguaging practices can be rooted in your instructional contexts. We hope these suggestions for professional development will assist you to both examine your beliefs and add to your instructional repertoire in teaching literacy to emergent bilingual students.

New Teacher Spotlight

We recognize that classroom teachers have different experience levels. Therefore, at scholastic.com/RootedResources, we provide "the essentials" to those who may be new to the profession and/or to the concepts in the chapter.

PART I

Translanguaging Into Literacy

▶ **VIDEO LINK**
You will find links to videos with the authors at scholastic.com/RootedResources.

CHAPTER 1

Translanguaging: Key Principles and New Possibilities

"Becoming biliterate is a journey, and journeys take time."

—BOBBIE KABUTO

We all hold theories about how reading and writing should be taught in general, and how they should be taught, specifically, to fit the needs of emergent bilinguals. Without a doubt, our theories impact our instruction. Some of us might think that reading in a new language begins with students learning the letters of the alphabet in order, engaging in isolated phonics exercises, or memorizing sight words. Others might think that reading and writing begin with the child's first literacy experiences at home, no matter in what language those experiences took place. Some might think that the role of the home language is crucial to becoming a reader and a writer until the child learns English. Still others might think that children can become readers and writers in two languages, but that this instruction must happen only in one language at a time if the child is to truly acquire a given named language. Traditionally, many educators believe that a child has to transition into English to be a full participant in classroom literacy practices. Rarely is students' bilingualism viewed as a strength that drives literacy. Our focus is on supporting and expanding students' *emerging* language practices as a means of engaging in literacy.

When we view literacy through a translanguaging lens, we acknowledge that bilingual or multilingual people creatively draw from their language and social resources to make meaning, regardless of the language they use. Educators can use translanguaging to create intentional literacy spaces in which students can creatively and critically use their resources to make meaning (García, 2020). The following is an example of how translanguaging exists as a resource as a child makes sense of a text. Carlos, a Latinx/Asian second grader, reads a book in Spanish about animals going to the river. At a turning point in the book, a wolf appears. Carlos says to himself, in English, "I love wolves!"—and then begins to howl. Carlos' engagement with text goes beyond simply translating the names of the animals in the book from Spanish to English. Rather, he forges an understanding of and connection to the book by speaking to himself in English about a story he read in Spanish. He also brings in a multimodal way of interacting with text by howling.

> *Bilingual or multilingual people creatively draw from their language and social resources to make meaning, regardless of the language they use.*

Carlos' translanguaging experience cuts to the core of literacy: the construction of meaning. Emergent bilinguals need to use all their linguistic practices to make sense of a text, to construct meaning, to learn, to express, and to reflect. Bilingualism must be the norm in our literacy classrooms as an important path to ensure all students can more fully participate in each learning experience we offer them. Translanguaging practices, after all, are the norm for bilingual individuals in bilingual communities (García & Kleyn, 2016).

Translanguaging Spaces in a Bilingual and Monolingual Classroom

Let's visit two classrooms where teachers actively weave translanguaging into their literacy instruction.

Translanguaging in a Bilingual Classroom

The children in this late-exit bilingual program class are engaged in a thematic study about plants and animals in the Arizona desert. Their teacher, Mary, has been reading fiction and nonfiction books to the children on those topics. On this day, Mary is reading aloud the book *The Desert Is My Mother/El desierto es mi madre* by Pat Mora (1994). During the read-aloud, Mary stops to ask the children to share with a partner what they've learned about the desert. She reminds them, in Spanish, "recuerden que pueden compartir con sus compañeros en inglés o en español. Lo que importa es que expliquen a su compañero/a lo que están aprendiendo sobre el desierto." [Remember that you can share with your classmates in

English or Spanish. What matters is that you explain what you are learning about the desert.]

José shares with his partner, "las plantas guardan el agua dentro de sus hojas [nopal pads] y tienen espinas." [Plants store the water in their leaves and they have thorns.] His partner shares his insights in Spanish with José. When it is time for partners to share with the whole group, Mary chooses José to share, who does so in Spanish. Mary asks for a volunteer to translate what José shared. Without hesitation, a volunteer translates his response.

After the read-aloud, Mary and the children talk about the ways in which plants, animals, and people live in the desert, in spite of it being hot and dry. She asks the children to think about how people might survive in the desert. A child recalls that the book *The Desert Is My Mother/El desierto es mi madre* said people eat "la tuna del cactus." Mary nods and opens the book to the page where it says that the desert gives people red prickly pears, or as the child explained in Spanish, "tunas." She asks the children if they have tried a prickly pear. She tells them she will look for it at the supermarket and bring it to the class.

During one of these experiences, Mary shares that in Mexico and in the Southwest, people also eat the leaves of the cactus. They are called "nopales." A few children relate that they, too, eat nopales at home, "nopales con huevo." Mary explains to the children that they will be cooking nopales on Friday with Juan's grandmother's help, so everyone can try them.

Translanguaging in a Monolingual Classroom

In another class—a general education, monolingual second-grade class—the children are studying point of view by examining two counter-narratives in fairy tales. They have read *Not Quite Snow White* by Ashley Franklin (2019) and today they read *Sulwe* by Lupita Nyong'o (2019). Mark, the teacher, selected those stories because he wants the children to see these counter-narratives of traditional fairy tales as the norm. He begins by engaging the children in the read-aloud. He asks them to describe the cover and predict what the story might be about. While reading aloud, he uses gestures, alters his voice to signal different characters, and points out the characters' actions. He stops at parts in the story and asks the children to make

predictions. He invites the children to discuss their thoughts, using their entire linguistic repertoire. Because Mark does not speak the children's named languages (20 percent speak Tagalog and 12 percent speak Chinese), he asks Adonis to translate the predictions the children share in Tagalog to English. At the end of the story, Mark invites the children to share their thoughts and questions about the two books. The children whose language is Tagalog or Chinese sit by other bilingual children, if possible. Mark takes notes on chart paper about what the children say.

Next, Mark tells the children that they will be doing a comparison of both stories with a particular focus on the characters in these non-traditional fairy tales. He holds up both books, reads the title of each one, and points to it on the cover. He asks the children to turn to a partner and share a similarity or difference between the two fairy tales.

He reminds them, once again, that they can use their entire linguistic repertoire to share.

Mark demonstrates for the children how they are going to use a Venn diagram to compare and contrast the stories. Pointing to each circle, he fills in the titles. He reminds the children that similarities between the fairy tales need to go in the middle, where the circles overlap. He asks a bilingual child to translate these directions. He demonstrates how partners will need to complete the handout he has prepared. Mark has planned strategically by pairing children who can communicate with each other. When Mark visits their table, the children explain in English the similarities and differences they find between the two fairy tales.

Although Mary and Mark are in different schools and in different programs, they both provide opportunities for students to use translanguaging to engage their students in content and to connect to others. They also demonstrate that children can translanguage naturally whether they are in a bilingual or monolingual classroom. Because the teachers provided opportunities for students to translanguage, everyone in the classroom community was involved in the conversation. The classes live out the principle that conversations that include the child's entire linguistic repertoire are foundational in the construction of meaning in literacy.

Students in classrooms that talk about translanguaging analyze how authors used words from named languages. [Translation: I think that the author wrote *challah* in another language because it is not a word in English or Spanish.]

Literacy Principles for Emergent Bilinguals

Ideally, you, as the teacher, will open spaces for emergent bilinguals to use translanguaging in intentional and purposeful ways. The personal sphere, school worlds, and languages of emergent bilinguals cannot and should not be kept separate. We advocate for a different vision in which bilingualism is the norm across diverse contexts and thus nurtures children's literacy development. These are the principles that guide our work:

- Listening, talking, reading, writing, and multiple modalities are tools for thinking, learning, wondering, and expressing that are central to the development of literacy(ies). To construct meaning fully, students need to leverage their entire linguistic repertoire in literacy events (e.g., reading, drawing, dramatizing, and talking about a poem).

- Students must have opportunities to engage with texts that allow them to participate in more complex and deeper thinking. Relying solely on the new language limits their ability to participate. In addition, children need access to texts that offer many perspectives and entry points.

- Students need to be involved right from the beginning in literacy events and be encouraged to engage as thoughtful and critical thinkers, readers, writers, and creators. Translanguaging allows this engagement in learning to happen.

- Translanguaging opens doors not only for students' linguistic repertoire, but also for families and communities' ways of knowing so they become partners in children's literacy development. Translanguaging builds connections between the worlds of school, family, and community.

How Can You Integrate Translanguaging Into Your Literacy Instruction?

There is not one way to start integrating translanguaging into your pedagogy as it can happen throughout the day and it can include all modes of language and expression (reading, listening, speaking, writing, viewing, gestures, audio recordings, images, and so on). Translanguaging can happen when a student reads a text quietly and makes notes. It can happen when a student talks with another student, or when the teacher talks to the class, or when students talk with one another. It can also happen when a student writes for a particular audience, for example a presentation to a group of parents or a thank-you letter to a presenter.

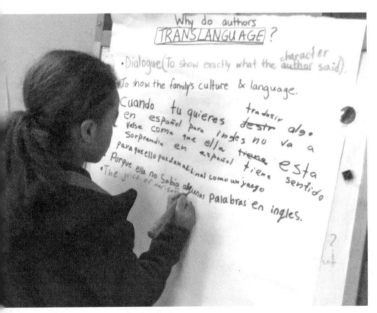

A student contributes to a group chart about how translanguaging can support literacy.

While translanguaging does happen naturally in the classroom, you also need to plan for it. You may pair students based on language background, for example, and have partners tackle a number of literacy tasks. If you give them a text in English, students may annotate it using their entire linguistic repertoire, including languages other than English. As students read with their partners, they can paraphrase, write a question, or state a connection in the language in which they are processing the material. Students can take the lead and share their discoveries in a language they understand best. You may also review a concept in the students' home language or ask a student to translate an idea for the class.

The purpose of literacy engagements matters. It is possible in our multilingual world that a student's final piece will be in a language different from the dominant one in the classroom. For example, if students are writing an invitation to a school event for parents, they might be working in small groups, brainstorming what to write in the invitation. The final invitation would match the language practices of the home. For example, students whose parents speak Arabic may choose to write in Arabic or include words in the invitation from their cultural and linguistic background. Composing the invitation in Arabic is an important literacy event, because it has a real use in the world and personal meaning.

Our starting point must be a pedagogy that normalizes bilingualism and positions bilinguals as people with strengths.

Translanguaging is a potent tool for constructing meaning, for thinking, for authentic communication and expression; it is not simply a scaffold to support students who are not yet fluent in English. It allows students to capitalize on their linguistic repertoire without rigid language boundaries.

The Next Step in Integrating Translanguaging Into Your Literacy Instruction

Translanguaging is based on what bilingual people do, how they use language, and how language serves their purposes. It begins with the learner. Therefore, our starting point must be a pedagogy that normalizes bilingualism and positions bilinguals as people with strengths.

To that end, we invite you to engage in the first two Actions. The first one, the Language Portrait, will deepen your understanding of your own language practices. The second one will help you explore how bilingualism exists in learning spaces.

Action 1

Create Your Own Language Portraits

Ofelia García, a lifelong bilingual educator and scholar, once spoke to a student who described his linguistic repertoire this way: "Spanish runs through my heart, but English rules my veins." The student precisely identifies how vital both languages are to his being. He could not survive without either of them. He also speaks to the unity between the two languages by suggesting that, together, they are the blood that flows through him.

This action asks you to identify how you live your languages and language practices. We start by asking you to inquire about your language practices, even if they match language considered the "standard" of school, by creating a language portrait: a biographical piece in which you map your named languages and language practices. Named languages are socially and politically constructed and are defined to belong to a nation or a state but do not represent how bilinguals language. In completing the "gingerbread" template below, consider the following:

- What named languages do I use? How did I learn them? Who do I use them with? When do I use these languages?

- What words and phrases do I use only in certain situations and with particular people?

- What language varieties (language practices that reflect my communities) do I speak? When and how do I use them?

Then assign your named languages and language practices a particular color to create a legend (see the example on the next page). Now, color your gingerbread template in a way that reflects the way that you live your languages and language practices.

For example, if your grandmother speaks Polish to you while you knit together, you can color the hands in the color you chose for Polish. If you and your Spanish-speaking mother are runners, color your legs the color that you chose for Spanish. Be as creative as possible. When you've finished your portrait, take some time to write about the decisions you made.

See Rebecca Quiñones's language portrait and written description on the following page to help guide you in creating your own. Notice at the bottom left, Rebecca has created a legend which links her chosen colors to her named languages and language practices, including Brooklyn English, English, Spanish, and Portuguese.

Rebecca wrote the following about her language portrait:

Even though my language portrait may seem complicated, I want to make clear that my solid language is English. I speak, read, write, count, and think in English most of the time. So much so that I included my Brooklyn English, my informal way of speaking. It is how I like to speak when I tell stories and make jokes with my friends. I'm very aware of my two "Englishes" because I need to turn them off and on consciously, depending on my current situation. I take pride in both ways I speak English because I feel like it makes me a versatile person.

In terms of Spanish, I learned it growing up from my grandparents, but not from my parents. Therefore, I am fluent, but I wouldn't consider it my first or my home language. Usually, I spoke Spanish with my grandparents, but now that I have friends in Argentina and I work with bilingual students in school, I find myself using Spanish much more often and in different ways. This is important to me because as I was growing up, I felt Spanish was leaving me, but after pursuing bilingual education, it's not only returning but also getting stronger.

I appreciate my languages because I see the role they play in my life in making my world bigger. I am trying to learn Portuguese because I want to learn a new "world" as well as be able to relate to students who have difficulty learning a new language.

(top) Language Portrait Template at scholastic.com/ RootedResources.

(right) Rebecca's language portrait

Rebecca tapped into her memories and patterns of how she uses language. She also makes clear the complexity of her language usage. In schools, sometimes we categorize students simplistically, but from Rebecca's example we learn that she, like other bilingual people, needs to capitalize on her complex linguistic repertoire daily and in intentional ways.

We invite you to fill out your own language portrait template and examine your language practices.

Action 2

Explore Translanguaging in a Classroom, Through a Student, or With a Colleague

To explore translanguaging practices, choose one or more of the following options:

1. Classroom Observation

Spend time in a classroom during literacy time and observe opportunities given to children for translanguaging. If you are a classroom teacher, think about your own classroom.

- What do you notice about the ways in which the teacher acknowledges and works from the children's diverse linguistic repertoires?

- In what ways does the teacher ensure that all the children understand what is being taught?

- How are directions provided? How is the particular content delivered? What languages are used throughout the lesson?

- Observe the children working at their seats. What kinds of interactions take place?

- What would it be like for a student for whom the named language is new to them to be in this classroom?

- What recommendations would you make to shift this classroom environment to a place where translanguaging is utilized to construct meaning?

Take some notes and, if possible, share with a colleague.

2. Observation of/Conversation With a Bilingual Child

Choose a bilingual child who interests you because he or she employs his or her bilingualism in novel ways or you want to delve deeper into the child's language practices. Observe him or her during regular class time, or during art or gym. How does this child use his bilingualism throughout the day? With whom? For what purposes? With older students, you might choose more than one bilingual student to observe. Ask them how they utilize their bilingualism when they read or write. When do they do it? For what purposes? If possible, share with your colleagues and ask for their feedback.

3. Teacher Interview

Interview a colleague informally about his or her beliefs about bilingualism. Ask:

- Can you tell me about your experiences learning and using other languages? How do you think these experiences help you understand your emergent bilinguals?

- Can you tell me about the students in your class? What is your class composition? How are the bilingual students labeled by your district or school? Have you ever heard of the term *emergent bilinguals*? What do you think it means?

- What strategies do you use to ensure that your emergent bilinguals can fully participate during literacy events? What would you like to do differently? In what additional ways do you support them?

- Can you describe how your classroom environment (physical, cognitive and socio-emotional) supports the emergent bilinguals in your class?

Closing Thoughts

In this chapter, we discussed the importance of beginning with the learner. For emergent bilinguals, translanguaging is the norm. It matters that we center the teaching of literacy(ies) on students' strengths by intentionally and purposefully planning for translanguaging. The first step in this journey is to reflect on your own language practices.

CHAPTER 2

Knowing Your Students and Creating a Multilingual Learning Environment

"Our teacher superpower is not some mythical teacher goodness or hyperbolic self-sacrifice.... Our superpower is listening, and there are several tools, attributes, and strategies that can augment our listening. If we listen to what children and communities are saying, and we respond accordingly, we can be ourselves again. We can be people. And if we can be people together, we'll discover that people can make things easier. We are all the answer that we'll ever need."

—CORNELIUS MINOR

The students in my (Laura's) second-grade Spanish/English dual-language bilingual classroom were from a mix of Latinx cultures. Many of my students were born in New York City but had rich and complex ties to the Dominican Republic, Puerto Rico, and Mexico. There were also students who were immigrants themselves from Ecuador, Guatemala, and Colombia and regularly communicated with family members in those countries. All of my students were immersed in their neighborhood communities, as well as the larger Brooklyn community.

All of those factors influenced the language that students used in the classroom. Here's an example from the beginning of the school year that showcases language diversity and how teachers' choices are critical to the flourishing of a dynamic and diverse linguistic repertoire in the classroom community. I asked my students to place their homework in their "mochilas," meaning "book bag" in the Colombian variety Spanish that I use. One student said, "Miss, pero eso es un bulto" [teacher, but that's a backpack]. Within the vast Spanish-speaking communities, Colombian variety Spanish is often considered "standard." Because of that, I could have said, "Well, it's called a mochila." However, I realized in that moment that my norm *should not stand in for that of my students'*. Reflecting on this experience and others, I learned that I could be intentional about my language use and pay attention to the ways in which my instructional decisions impacted my students' understanding of how their language practices are welcome in school and enrich it.

The way that one listens to children is also impacted by their racial backgrounds, social identities, and the power relationships that stem from them (Rosa & Flores, 2017). As teachers, we must interrogate and develop counter-ideologies to make sure we don't deprecate or suppress the language practices of emergent bilinguals as we forge equitable language practices.

Expanding the Students' Linguistic Repertoire

After the "mochila" experience, my students and I started an ongoing dictionary of synonyms in Spanish. The entries were wide-ranging and stemmed from things we used in the classroom. For example, for "tape," I used "cinta pegante," while my Dominican students used the word "teipi." This wasn't just an academic exercise to identify synonyms, but rather a way to recognize the varieties of Spanish that my students used in their families and communities. Highlighting the language that students actively used shifted the tone of the classroom by welcoming students' actual language practices. It also enriched and expanded the students' and teachers' language practices.

Teachers can support students to create resources which highlight the diversity of ways of saying a single word. Fifth grader Matteo creates a visual for different words in Spanish for the word "kite."

Our students are immersed in a web of language from the moment they are born. Language binds us together. Students' language practices are so ingrained in who they are that they are often not even aware of them. If students' home language practices match those at school, their transition to school may be seamless. However, if there is a difference between students' language practices at home and school, you need to embrace a stance that respects the language practices that students possess, while building and expanding upon them. Even if you share named languages with your students, you must be aware of the messages about language you send, because teachers, regardless of their background, are the first to usher students into school language environments.

In addition, we concur with Cioè-Peña (2020) and Martínez-Álvarez (2019), whose work centers on emergent bilinguals with the socially constructed label "disabled" and their right to bilingual education. As Cioè-Peña (2020) advocates, "All linguistically diverse children have a right to learn in their home language in order to be able to access basic human rights within their communities and their families" (p. 4). The richest literacy environment for all emergent bilinguals—regardless of race, economic background, language background, and learning abilities—is one in which bilingualism and/or multilingualism is the norm.

In the spirit of Genishi and Haas-Dyson (2009), understanding emergent bilinguals' diverse language backgrounds is crucial to instruction because it embraces "the normalcy of difference" (p. 145). This contradicts the idea that language differences are often thought of as a challenge rather than as a necessary and important part of deepening the learning process for all. It also contradicts the idea that all children, regardless of their backgrounds and educational history, need to be in the same place academically to be ready for school.

Furthermore, the number of emergent bilinguals is on the rise, and where they live is shifting from major cities and along the borders to suburban and rural areas (Batalova & McHugh, 2010; Sugarman & Geary, 2018). Emergent bilinguals make up an eclectic group. They vary in country of birth, languages spoken, ethnicity, race, educational background, socioeconomic class, learning abilities and disabilities, among other features. Yet, despite the incredible diversity of emergent bilinguals, they are often grouped together and regarded as having the same needs. Regretfully, they are also usually viewed through a deficit lens. In other words, misguided educators may believe that emergent bilinguals do not "have" English, nor do they understand the intricacies of what it means to be successful in an American school. This perspective prevents teachers from building on students' bilingual strengths and resources.

Rather than moving from one point to the next in a straight line, students' language learning is interactive, integrated, and dynamic.

Because emergent bilinguals are so different from each other—and in your classroom they will change from one year to the next—our advocacy is strong and clear. To you we say:

- Be curious and open-minded about the emergent bilinguals in your classroom.
- Acknowledge that emergent bilinguals are all different and diverse—in terms of race, ethnicity, educational background, learning profiles, socioeconomic status, geographical background, etc. Diversity among emergent bilinguals is the norm.
- Start from a perspective of strength.
- Avoid deficit views. If you do find yourself making them, investigate why.

Regarding that last point, deficit statements such as "These students do not have language" and "They can't speak any language" reflect a stance that language development in school is acceptable only when it's linear and/or standardized. These statements position some students as poised for success and others as "already behind" before they even step through the front door. If we view students' language in this way, we restrict access and deny opportunities.

Our stance posits just the opposite: students develop language dynamically. That means rather than moving from one point to the next in a straight line, students' language learning is interactive, integrated, and dynamic. To develop as language learners, children need to capitalize on their entire linguistic repertoire. They need to develop language through interaction with a diverse set of peers and adults and within a variety of contexts.

Action 3

Get to Know Your Emergent Bilingual Students

In his groundbreaking book, *Writing: Teachers & Children at Work* (1983), Donald Graves asks teachers to write down frequently everything they know about their students. He posits that the student that is difficult to teach is the one that is not known. Writing down everything he knew about each of his students enabled Graves to identify those he knew a lot about versus those he needed to learn about. Cappellini (2005), Celic (2009), and Espinosa, Ascenzi-Moreno, and Vogel (2016) emphasize the importance of knowing emergent bilingual students, specifically becoming familiar with their language abilities and histories.

This action is informed by the work of all of those educators. We ask you to develop a portrait of each student. First, on a copy of the chart below, write the names of all your students as they occur to you. Then write all of their interests and what you know generally about each one, focusing on positive traits and resources, rather than perceived shortcomings. Next, write the languages that they regularly use and country of origin. Once you remember what you know about each student off the "top of your head," you can more easily identify students that you need to get to know better.

Getting to Know My Students

Name	Interests, Traits, Resources	Language(s)	Country of Origin	Knowledge of Language Practices
Sofia	Soccer Science Plants	English Spanish	Ecuador	Speaks Spanish to friends and family. Connections to weather and nature. Traditional songs from Ecuador. Chatting platforms.
Alex	Soccer Video games Pottery Baking	English Spanish Italian	Student: U.S. Parents: Colombia Italy	Speaks mostly English. Speaks Spanish and Italian to grandmothers. Video games. YouTubers. Chatting platforms. Soccer stats.
Joseph	Soccer Skateboarding Comics	English Spanish Garifuna	Student: U.S. Parents: Guatemala	Speaks Spanish to parents, some knowledge of Garifuna, English. Comics. Skateboarding-specific terms and words.

Find a blank form online at scholastic.com/RootedResources.

Creating a Linguistic Landscape for Emergent Bilinguals

The ways in which language is experienced in schools—whether across the environment or via the members of the school community—is referred to as linguistic landscape. Paying attention to the linguistic landscape of your school is important because it sends a powerful message to students and families that their languages and linguistic repertoires are valued. Additionally, an accurate linguistic landscape—one that truly matches the languages of the children at school—serves as an important resource to emergent bilingual students (Menken, Pérez Rosado, & Guzman Valerio, 2018). You can design your classroom environment to reflect the language practices of your students and expose your students to language practices other than their own.

> *Paying attention to the linguistic landscape of your school is important because it sends a powerful message to students and families that their languages and linguistic repertoires are valued.*

In the Primary Grades

Imagine the kindergarten classroom designed by Daisy. She knows that all of her students come to school with language differences, as well as a range of understandings about literacy. Because of that, Daisy has set up the classroom to connect to her students' lived experiences, knowing that in order to extend those experiences and their language, she needs to build from them. On the outside of the classroom door, she posted all the children's names as well as the words, "Welcome!," "¡Bienvenidos!," and "欢迎" (in Mandarin). At first glance, Daisy's classroom looks like many rich early-childhood learning environments. However, when you take a closer look, you can see that it is attuned to the diversity of learners in her classroom. The children's literature on display represents and extends beyond the diversity of her students. Kid-favorite audiobooks recorded in Spanish and Mandarin by parents are available. Daisy has also asked parents to provide clothes and props that represent their cultures and home lives. Students are invited to wear those, along with traditional dress-up clothes, such as a doctor's white coat and a firefighter's helmet.

Daisy also knows that students arrive at her classroom with a variety of language experiences. So, she spends time getting to know them holistically by providing them with a wide range of materials and experiences. As they play, she engages them to understand their language practices, as well as to provide them with opportunities to expand their language facility. For instance, in the block area, she posts pictures of the Mexican panadería, the Korean fruit store, and store signs in English, Russian, and Chinese. As she plays with the children, she listens for when they naturally translanguage and encourages them to express their ideas.

Beyond the Primary Grades

A rich linguistic landscape isn't just the hallmark of the primary grades. No matter what grade you teach, make sure all classroom print—from your welcome signs to your anchor charts—reflects the multilingual spectrum represented in your classroom. For example, you can develop and support a rich, diverse schoolscape by posting student work in different languages. Additionally, provide spaces for students to work (orally and in writing) using their entire linguistic repertoire across the curriculum. Create powerful reference charts, such as multilingual word walls, to support students' participation and engagement in your classroom inquiry. Developing a purposeful, multilingual space is important for a variety of reasons. First, it establishes that in your classroom and, ideally, your school, the languages of students and families are valued. Second, with multilingual labels and explanations, it provides students and families with easy access to essential school information. Last, a linguistic landscape needs to support and extend student engagement with the learning concepts at hand.

Administrators can ensure that the school building as a whole and classrooms within it have rich schoolscapes by setting the right tone and providing resources. Menken, et al. (2018) recommend creating resource packets for parents in multiple languages and showcasing in classrooms and school libraries books that reflect the building's multiple home languages.

Think about the classroom spaces that you provide for your students' diverse language practices and the things you could do to recognize their language practices and build upon them.

Action 4

Explore Your Language Ecology

Look around at the print in your community at large. What languages are featured in newspapers, restaurant signs, radio stations, and so forth? When you walk into your school, what languages do you see? How do these languages match or not match the languages of members of the school community? Now take a look at your classroom. What languages and linguistic repertoires are featured there? How are they featured?

We ask you to analyze the language ecology of your classroom. Ecology, in biology, refers to the study of the relationships between living organisms, including humans. In our case, we refer to language ecology as the relationship between a person's language practices and the language environment that surrounds the child. Language ecology refers to how language practices are present in both the physical and lived environment for the speaker to thrive in that environment. The languages featured in school and classroom environments send a critical message to parents and

students about what is valued. Consider the following: Maspeth, Queens, in New York City, is a Polish neighborhood. If you were to walk around the neighborhood, you would see signs in both Polish and English, you would find newspapers in both languages, and you would hear people speaking English, Polish, and other languages that New Yorkers use. However, as soon

A multilingual bulletin board welcomes parents who speak a variety of languages to school by offering translations of common questions.

as you walk into the neighborhood's school, all print and conversation would be in English. There is no Polish or Spanish, the other named language spoken in the neighborhood. What message do you think parents and students take away from this mismatch? When emergent bilinguals step into a school building that features only English, it may signal that they must leave their linguistic repertoire, which includes their home languages, at the door. The same holds true for their parents. Consider the following:

1. You are a parent who speaks a language other than English, and you are about to enter the school.

   - How would you feel walking in?

   - Who could you speak to?

   - How would you communicate your needs?

2. Look around your classroom and think about how your students experience it.

   - How does it reflect the languages and lives of your students?

   - How are your students with varied language abilities able to access resources, engage with peers, and participate fully in instruction?

   - What materials do you have (books, magazines, etc.), and how do they reflect and extend your students' language practices?

   - What are some areas in your room that could be opened up for multilingualism? Why and how?

   - What materials do you have that represent the language diversity of current students and future students?

After reflecting on these questions, draw a map of your school and your classroom, indicating how either a parent or child with limited English would navigate through them. Where would they be able to get information? What spaces can become more multilingual?

Think deeply about your emergent bilinguals and how they experience the language ecology that you have created. In this way, you can shift the language ecology in favor of a more accurate representation of your students and the communities.

Closing Thoughts

Getting to know your students is a critical first step in addressing their needs. And getting to know your emergent bilinguals requires you to not only learn about them as language learners, but also understand them as they are connected to their families and rooted in their communities. We urge you to not only get to know your students, but also to value their knowledge and build on their funds of knowledge as essential components of your teaching.

Suggestions for Professional Development

These suggested professional development questions center on how bilingualism and biliteracy exists in the school community, as well as the language ecology in your school and classrooms.

1   With a partner or in a small group, walk around your school's neighborhood. Take photos of literacy moments in different settings. For example, capture signs for the different businesses, advertisements, and newspapers. Go inside a restaurant and examine the menus. Consider the languages in which the print is written. Once you return to school, get together with your team. Share what you learned about the community's linguistic practices. What did you learn about the community and its linguistic resources? Did anything surprise you? Share your photo essay with the rest of your school colleagues. As a large group, make a list of the community's linguistic practices and its resources. What are its linguistic strengths?

2   Walk around the school with two or three colleagues and photograph its language ecology. Then examine your photos, thinking about the status of the language ecology for all children at the school. What is missing? How could it be enhanced? Could you develop a survey to identify the linguistic landscape of the school? Then, with other small groups, present your findings to the rest of the school staff. With all groups, combine findings and develop a plan of action to ensure that the school's language ecology reflects the children's, teachers', staff members', and families' linguistic repertoires. Think about how your linguistic landscape could be made visible. Perhaps you and a team of colleagues, parents, and students could paint a mural or create a bulletin board or display

that welcomes everyone and makes the languages of the school visible. What signs are needed in the school in languages other than English? How do these signs enable the families to navigate the building and grounds?

3 Draw a map of your ideal classroom's language ecology. As you consider the children in your class, what should this map look like? Share your map with a group of colleagues. Talk to a colleague about ways of incorporating these ideas into your classroom space.

Fifth-grade teacher Cindy Quiroz ensures that her classroom environment features images and signs that are multilingual and diverse to affirm her students' identities.

PART II

Reading Into Meaning

VIDEO LINK
You will find links
to videos with
the authors at
scholastic.com/
RootedResources.

CHAPTER 3

The Reading Process for Emergent Bilinguals

"Bilingual readers leverage all of their meaning-making resources and all of themselves as they engage with text. Some of these resources are linguistic and verbal; others are visual; others involve gestures, the body, as well as the lives and knowledge systems with which speakers have engaged."

—OFELIA GARCÍA

In Part I, we proposed a way of thinking about emergent bilinguals' languages, literacies, and resources, and how to capitalize on them in your classroom. In Part II, we apply a translanguaging framework to the teaching of reading. We discuss how the reading process exists and unfolds for emergent bilinguals and the types of practices you can put in place to reflect robust notions of bilingualism and biliteracy.

Reading is a process. However, many teachers focus on children's reading levels, at the expense of their interests, their expertise in various areas, or the reading strategies they need to learn. When we focus exclusively on reading levels, we do not take into account who the child is as a reader and how the child navigates the text. Instead, our sole focus—and, too often, the children's sole focus—is on moving from level to level, without ever considering if there is a topic they are passionate about or a genre they love.

We learn to gauge our effectiveness as reading teachers primarily on how students progress through levels.

However, while making progress across text complexity is critical to a child's reading development and identity, so are engagement, thinking, knowledge of an author's body of work, knowledge of particular genres, curiosity about a topic, ability to talk with others about texts. Don't get us wrong, we want all students to develop their skills and abilities increasingly to become engaged, critical readers. Reading is a process and not a linear progression. And because of that, the pathway for each reader will be varied and diverse. For emergent bilingual readers, the process is impacted by language(s) and cultural resources that students bring to the table.

Reading as a Unified and Complex Process

Reading weaves together psychological, sociocultural, and linguistic processes (Kabuto, 2017). With that fact in mind, we propose replacing the outdated notion that students develop as readers in English and a language other than English separately. Instead, we propose that readers develop by drawing upon the full span of their resources, including their home and other languages, often in a synergistic, interwoven way (Ascenzi-Moreno, 2016; García & Kleifgen, 2019; García, 2020). When young children begin to read, they bring to the process their lived experiences (schemas); their emergent knowledge of books, letters, and sounds; and the conversations they have participated in at home and in their communities to make meaning (K. Goodman, 1996; K. Goodman & Y. Goodman, 2014). While the National Reading Panel (2000) identifies five pillars of reading instruction—phonemic awareness, phonics, fluency, vocabulary, and comprehension—this view does not provide the whole picture because it separates competencies into discrete skills. Reading experts caution us about that view; comprehension must frame all components of reading to ensure that instruction is meaningful (Taberski, 2010).

Allyn and Morrell (2015) go further by rooting reading to students' contexts. Strong readers develop within communities of readers. This is why it matters that we take the time to create a classroom community that values reading and who the readers are. This happens by viewing the child as a human being and ensuring that reading is meaningful to him or her. In sum, as children learn to read and understand what it means to be a reader, they integrate their understanding of the world, words, texts, images, and language to engage with texts and develop deeper meanings.

As educators, we must envision the kinds of readers we need for a future in which multilingualism is the norm. Beers and Probst (2017) write, "Words matter in a democracy, and thus it is vitally important that all members of the society respect and attend closely to them" (p. 162). They add, "Ultimately, we are teaching children to read the text of their own lives. We want them open to possibility, open to ideas, open to new evidence that encourages a change of opinion" (p. 163). We ask, what are the qualities in readers that we need for a more multilingual, interconnected, and globalized world?

Reading as a Dynamic Process

Reading does not start with teaching students the letter *a*, but rather with the texts that surround them at home, such as environmental print (which often comes in the languages of the community), daily mail, notes from and by family members, conversations among family members, digital tools used in the household, as well as other ways of experiencing print. In some families, books and other literacy resources, such as recorded songs and language-based play experiences, abound. In other families, oral stories and playful poetic language are more common. Despite those differences, we must embrace a broad definition of reading, and recognize children's experiences and strengths. Our ideas about the reading process shape nearly every instructional decision we make in our classrooms.

Reading does not start with teaching students the letter a, but rather with the texts that surround them at home.

Our reading instruction must not be static nor "one size fits all." We must draw upon our knowledge and resources about the reading process to support and challenge our students. We also draw on our own experiences as readers, since these often inform how we teach reading. When it comes to emergent bilingual students, we must understand how their rich linguistic repertoire impacts and influences their development as readers. Our pedagogy must start with the whole child and how he or she interacts with text.

These ideas are not new. Louise Rosenblatt (1978) coined the idea of reading as a transaction—a transaction that is carried out between the reader and the text, within a particular instance. For example, the first time I (Cecilia) read Mario Vargas Llosa's *La Fiesta del Chivo* (*The Goat's Feast*) I considered it the story of a dictator in a faraway land. After I visited the Dominican Republic and worked with New York City bilingual teachers who come from the Dominican Republic, I reread Vargas Llosa's book and viewed it very differently because of my new personal experiences. Now I knew the people whose families were deeply affected by the actions of Trujillo, a Dominican dictator.

From Rosenblatt's (1978) perspective, the text is just marks on paper until a reader engages with it. She argued vehemently for a transactional view of reading. Meaning lies in the interaction between the text and the reader. The reader's prior experiences impact the construction of meaning, which is why no two readers will walk away with the same understanding of the same text, nor have the same experience.

More recently, K. Goodman and Y. Goodman (2014), Harvey and Goudvis (2017), Allyn and Morrell (2015), Goodman and Fries (2016), and Beers and Probst (2017) have urged teachers to define reading as thinking, as the construction of meaning, and as social enactment. The reader is not passive, but active and in charge of his or her own agency. We need to keep in mind also that who we are as readers changes as our experiences shift and as we read about familiar topics more deeply or read about new topics. As Tara Westover describes in her memoir *Educated* (2018), readers develop their voice in relation to both the texts and the people that usher them through the reading process. She writes, "My life was narrated for me by others. Their voices were forceful, emphatic, absolute. It had never occurred to me that my voice might be as strong as theirs" (Westover, 2018, p. 197).

We want all of our students, including emergent bilinguals, to grow as readers with the deep understanding that they are agents of the reading process, with strong voices. For the youngest emergent bilinguals, reading is also a transactional process. Young children need reading experiences. While they are learning to read, they need ample opportunities to interact with others (teachers, family members, classmates). Books, words, and stories come alive when connected to memories of being read to or reading along with others, as well as discussing those books, words, and stories with others. Talk deepens their understanding of texts. When children live in a world of print and languages, they become familiar with the words around them.

When children live in a world of print and languages, they become familiar with the words around them.

Reading for emergent bilinguals does not mean reading in one language or another or transitioning to reading in only one language. Emergent bilinguals should be encouraged to use the full span of their linguistic and cultural resources to engage in reading. For example, while a student may read a book in English about going to the market, he may recall in Chinese experiences of going to different types of markets. The child might also share in Chinese the names of some vegetables with a partner. If the teacher invites the child to share his or her thinking using his or her entire linguistic repertoire, it will likely be a richer and deeper experience than if the child shared only in English. Teaching this way allows the student to connect to the reading process in multifaceted ways.

For emergent bilinguals, the reading process should not be divided into English reading and reading in another language. It is a *unified* process. If we see reading from an internal perspective—as it exists for the reader—we see more clearly that reading is not partitioned into various named languages. García (2020) writes, "Even though the teacher, in what she or he imagines is an English-language classroom, may be viewing instruction only through English and restricting other languages, bilingual students need to orchestrate, and are in fact orchestrating, all their multilingual/multimodal resources in the act of reading a text" (p. 558). Emergent bilinguals, regardless of the type of program they are in, are developing biliteracy, which is, at its heart, a meaning-making process that involves reading and writing across languages and modalities (Hornberger & Link, 2012).

As you read the rest of this book, we invite you to reimagine reading and writing from the perspective of children and how they bring together all of their resources to make meaning and enjoy text. Regardless of the grade you teach, or the students you have, one of your first teaching steps is to create an intentional reading environment that is rooted in emergent bilinguals' strengths. In the following section, we discuss how setting the stage for learning can shift when you take a translanguaging perspective to create a linguistically rich and welcoming environment.

The Reading Environment From a Translanguaging Perspective

Creating a reading environment where multilingualism is the norm is critical. One of the first steps is to ensure that your classroom contains resources that reflect your students' languages and cultures. Those resources should include the print around the room, such as posters and anchor charts, as well as books that are read to students and to which they have access. The classroom should also contain reading materials written in the languages the children speak, such as fiction and nonfiction texts, environmental print, songs, poems, magazines, and student- and teacher-made announcements.

Lastly, it is important to understand what home literacies exist and to value them, even if they are unfamiliar to you. For example, I (Laura) grew up in a home that was rich in oral language but contained very few books. For many educators, that may sound an alarm that I was in danger of missing out on a literate life or falling behind even before going to school. However, my life was rich and quite literate because of the stories I heard while walking to the fruit store and before falling asleep. It's critical for teachers to value all types of literacies, even if they do not match those the school values.

Ways to Create a Multilingual Reading Landscape

Display:

- photographs of various places in the community and maps (local, world)

- children's writing in all their languages

- teacher-made charts (classroom community–generated)

- books in a variety of genres (e.g., poetry, nonfiction, fiction). To the best of your ability, make sure they represent the students' language backgrounds.

Embracing Diverse Children's Literature

One way to link students' home and school lives is by gathering diverse, multilingual children's literature. Here, we discuss how children's literature can expand horizons in your classroom to create a rich multilingual reading environment.

The landscape of children's literature is constantly changing. While more books with diverse characters are being released, these types of books still do not parallel the U.S. population at large (Henderson, Warren, Whitmore, Seely Flint, Tropp Laman, & Jaggers, 2020; Lee & Low, 2019). Teachers must make conscientious and continual efforts to stay abreast of the literature available so that their classroom libraries are filled with books that are culturally and linguistically relevant and sustaining.

Rudine Sims Bishop (1990) calls upon teachers to offer books that serve as "mirrors" and "windows." She writes, "Literature transforms human experience and reflects it back to us and in that reflection we can see our own lives and experiences as part of the larger human experience" (1). In other words, Sims Bishop notes the importance of books containing characters and experiences that children can intimately relate to, as well as books that open wide entire new worlds. Since Sims Bishop's call, the need for books that reflect the identities of children from diverse communities has become even more urgent (España & Herrera, 2020; Lee & Low, 2019; Lehner-Quam, West, & Espinosa, 2020).

In Chapter 2, we invited you to examine the children in your class, the languages they speak, and the resources that they bring. Now, use that knowledge to think about the kinds of stories and books that reflect their experiences. Janelle Henderson, an elementary school teacher who challenges other teachers to interrogate their classroom libraries,

This English as a New Language (ENL) teacher offers her students books in a variety of languages, which contributes to a rich multilingual environment.

pushes our thinking (Henderson et al., 2020). She notes that while it is commendable to have, for example, books with Black characters, it is our responsibility to make sure that those characters reflect the diversity of our students' personalities and lived experiences. She reminds us how important it is to resist accepting classroom libraries that we inherit, and instead constantly inquire about and search for books that actively reflect a range of identities and support students in seeing both themselves and others.

Ways to Interrogate Your Classroom Library

When you engage in this process of interrogating your classroom library, ask yourself:

- Who is depicted in the books that you read aloud to children and that they read on their own? Think about the characters in books along multiple dimensions (gender, sex, race, identity, personality, etc.). How are they depicted? Are they represented in simplistic or complex ways?

- When students choose books, do they have access to books that depict kids like them in complex ways?

- When students choose books, do they have access to books that depict diverse people across the United States in complex ways?

- How are characters who speak languages other than English depicted in the books?

Once you've considered the books you have and the books you would like to have, you need to locate the latter. How do you begin? Look for books that have won awards from a wide range of reputable committees and organizations. By reputable, we mean committees and organizations that not only examine children's books for their quality, but also for their contribution to expanding the diversity of characters and content. The following list of committees and organizations, while not exhaustive, can help you begin to search for books that serve as mirrors and windows for the children in your classroom. We want to highlight the Pura Belpré Award, which focuses on Latinx authors writing about the Latinx experience. Winners of this award celebrate multilingualism for Spanish-English bilinguals.

Looking for Books? Start Here!

- **We Need Diverse Books** diversebooks.org
- **Pura Belpré Award** ala.org/alsc/awardsgrants/bookmedia/belpremedal
- **Coretta Scott King Award** ala.org/rt/emiert/cskbookawards
- **America's Award** claspprograms.org/americasaward
- **Schneider Family Book Award** ala.org/awardsgrants/schneider-family-book-award
- **Jane Addams Peace Association** janeaddamschildrensbookaward.org
- **American Indians in Children's Literature** americanindiansinchildrensliterature.blogspot.com/p/best-books.html
- **Charlotte Huck Award** ncte.org/awards/ncte-childrens-book-awards/charlotte-huck-award
- **Orbis Pictus Award** ncte.org/awards/orbis-pictus-award-nonfiction-for-children
- **NCTE Award for Excellence in Poetry for Children** ncte.org/awards/excellence-in-poetry-for-children-living-american-poet

Establishing Routines and Expectations

It's important that daily routines and expectations for your students are written in the languages they speak, and perhaps also with pictures to convey key ideas. If the schedule is predictable, the routines clear, and the reading environment student-centered, emergent bilinguals will take ownership and be able to exercise fully their agency during reading time. Remember, reading the daily routines is a way to support children's literacy development in authentic, purposeful ways. Reading is reading, regardless of the language in which it is done.

Preparing for and Managing Reading Time

Here are some questions to help you reflect on the way you prepare for and manage reading time.

- How do I want to organize the reading time and how will it best support my students?

- What do I know about how my emergent bilingual students read, and based on this understanding, how can I support emergent bilinguals as they read?

- What are my students' practices outside of school?

- In what languages do the readers in the community read?

- What do you want to share with the emergent bilingual children about what you value about the reading practices you want them to develop in your class?

- In what ways do these practices contribute, sustain, and celebrate the children's multilingualism?

- In what languages do you need to offer the children reading material?

Emergent Bilinguals as Emergent Readers

It is important to distinguish between the terms *emergent bilingual readers* and *emergent readers* in general. Emergent bilingual readers are children who are learning to read in two or more languages, regardless of their developmental phase. Emergent readers are children who are gaining knowledge about what it means to be a reader and that reading holds meaning while they are developing concepts of print. Over time, they will develop knowledge about sounds, letters, and words, always starting with what's important to them.

This section is about emergent bilingual readers, who, no doubt, have had rich experiences with text, often in various named languages, from a very early age.

Where Does Reading Begin?

Children are cradled in oral language and print. Beginning at birth, most of them participate in and hear conversations around them from important people in their lives. Through those conversations, they hear stories that are told to them and read to them. How children learn to talk about those stories can vary, depending on the sociocultural contexts of their family. What is important for us educators to remember is that, in all families, there is richness of language.

The literacy practices around print are multimodal and differ, depending on the sociocultural and linguistic practices of the family. Language practices are clearly part of a family's funds of knowledge

Three-year-old Rosaly enjoys one of her favorite bilingual books.

(Moll, Amanti, Neff, & González, 1992; López-Robertson, 2017). Children are also surrounded by music, TV images and sounds, street signs, advertisements, digital media, books, and other forms of communication. There are many pathways to learning language. Emergent bilingual children come from homes in which authentic literacy practices serve the family's purposes, and many of those practices are carried out in a variety of languages. Family members engage in translanguaging or use resources from a variety of named languages.

Students and their families study butterflies in their home languages. They create a butterfly collage in both English and Spanish. Students' final writing about butterflies is in English.

Emergent bilingual children learn early on that print has function and purpose (to advertise, to advise, to show, to inspire, to share feelings, to help the reader figure out how to do something, and to argue, among others). They, often with their parents, are continually reading their environment and interacting with it. The print is often in a variety of languages to serve particular purposes and needs in the community. Children observe their parents engaged in authentic literacy events daily, ranging from reading the newspaper, to finding out what's on sale at the supermarket, to taking in information for their jobs. They might observe their parents reading a text on their phone in a language other than English. They might observe them reading the news in English but talking about it in a language other than English.

There are many pathways to learning language.

Family literacy practices are not static but instead evolve based on need, purpose, and access to resources (smartphones and computers, for example). We must start with an understanding that children come to school with language practices that were developed within families and communities, and their backgrounds may be different from what we typically value in school.

Into the Classroom

Exploring Environmental Print

It is the beginning of the school year. Mr. Lee asks the children in his first-grade class if they know how to read. Only a few hands go up. He reminds the children that he thinks everyone is a reader and that he has a way of showing them. Mr. Lee takes the children on a walk around the community to examine its environmental print. During the walk, he talks to the children about the purpose of signs they notice: a stop sign, a stoplight, a crossing street sign, one- way and two-way street signs, the school's entry sign, no parking signs, etc. He also takes photographs of these signs. The next day, Mr. Lee

asks the children again if they think they are readers. He shares a slide presentation of the photographs he took the day before. He asks the children to read with him each sign as it is projected and explain its meaning. To ensure that everyone fully participates, he pairs up students to translate for one another, as necessary. For example, he partners Joaquín, who speaks Spanish at home, with Silvia, who speaks mostly English with her family. Joaquín shares in Spanish that the sign with an arrow means "una vía," and then Silvia translates "una vía" to English, "one way." At the end of the session, Mr. Lee reminds the

Teachers can support students' awareness of environmental print at home by asking them to send in pictures of food labels in different languages found in their homes.

children that they are all readers. He then tells the children they will create a bilingual class book about signs. He again pairs them carefully and gives partners a sign to draw and write about. This book will become part of the classroom library.

Next, Mr. Lee writes a letter to parents, asking them to send in empty boxes for items the family buys often, such as cereal, beans, and cookies. He also asks them to take a walk with their children in the neighborhood and take pictures of the print they see. His aim is to encourage the families to closely examine how print exists in the world. In the classroom, he will ask the children to share their noticings, and he will create a new learning experience with environmental print by displaying the text in the artifacts and photos the children bring that illustrates for everyone that they are all readers, and that print exists everywhere. In creating this experience, Mr. Lee wants to ensure that the classroom environment reflects the print that exists in the communities in which the children live, as well as the fact that in many cases, texts in these communities exist in multiple languages.

Early childhood teachers are often encouraged to place great value on alphabetic knowledge when children enter school. The rich knowledge about literacy that emergent bilinguals bring to school, and how it exists in their particular multilingual communities, is often overlooked. As a result, emergent bilinguals are frequently viewed as empty vessels or, worse, incapable of becoming successful readers and writers. As teachers of young emergent bilinguals, we want to capitalize on the knowledge emergent bilingual children bring with them.

Early childhood teacher Nikki Laugier ensures the representation of both English and Spanish in her dual-language bilingual virtual classroom setup.

As we stated in Chapter 2, teachers should pay attention to the linguistic landscape of the classroom because it sends a powerful message to families and students that their language practices are valued. Also, when familiar linguistic and social practices are present, they serve as starting places for children's literacy development.

Action 5

Examine Environmental Print in Your Classroom

Classrooms are small communities that showcase cultural norms through the print on display. For example, many elementary teachers post welcome signs on the door in English only, even if their students speak languages other than English. We believe the environmental print of your classroom should be multilingual, capturing the languages of all your students. Environmental print is one way young readers begin to read through their lived experiences in the classroom. At the heart of that action is the question, "What message do I want to send to the children and their families about the language ecology of my classroom?"

Here are some questions to consider when you think about environmental print and your students' languages and social resources.

- Are labels in your classroom in English and a language other than English?

- In dual-language bilingual classrooms, do the resources in the home languages have an equal presence with the resources in English? Are there resources in the languages of children who speak a language other than the target languages? (For example, in a Spanish-English dual-language bilingual program, it is possible that children who speak Albanian attend. Are there resources in Albanian, in addition to Spanish and English?)

- In monolingual classrooms, are there resources in languages other than English?

- Does the work posted on bulletin boards reflect the languages of the students in your classroom and the broader school community?

As you consider these questions, take a tour of your classroom, starting with the door and moving to the walls—the bulletin boards (including the titles and children's work), anchor charts, posters; parent corner; books in the library; student materials on the desks; labels on objects, materials, and furniture. The chart on the following page may help you.

Multilingual Analysis of Classroom Environmental Print

Classroom Feature	How does this feature contribute to a multilingual print environment?	What are some ways to incorporate multilingualism?
Classroom Door	It's the first thing that students, parents, faculty, and visitors see and sets the tone for the classroom.	Welcome greeting in different languages Pictures of diverse book covers on the door
Titles of Bulletin Boards	Normalizes multilingualism of students' work featured for the classroom community	Use bilingual titles on bulletin boards.
Posters & Photos (children, families, the community)	Serves as a reference or affirmation for students	Put up bilingual posters and pictures and/or posters in languages that students use.
Teacher-Made Anchor Charts to Support Content Areas	Serves as a multilingual reference tool for students	Create bilingual/multilingual anchor charts.
Student Resources on Desk	Provides students with resources to support their work	Provide students with bilingual dictionaries (with pictures). Provide students with frequently used words and phrases in English and other languages that students use.
Materials around the Room (e.g., books in different genres and languages, including books written by children in the class)	Provides access to a classroom library that is inclusive of diverse authors, which includes the children themselves, and features diverse language practices	Ensure these are representative of multilingualism of the children and their families.
Classroom Passes	Normalizes multilingualism around the school	Make school passes multilingual.
Labels for objects, materials, class areas, content-area stations, class jobs, calendar, weather, and furniture	Provides a reference for students of classroom features Normalizes bilingualism in the classroom	Post labels for objects, materials, and furniture in both English and the languages that students use. Provide labels for content areas in multiple languages.
Send-Home Letters to Caregivers	Provides information to all caregivers, regardless of the language they use Sends the message to everyone that they are included in the classroom community	Send letters to caregivers in the languages they use.
Word walls and content area–specific displays	Give students access to key words in multiple languages	Provide translations and definitions of key words in the languages that students use.
Family Corner	Provides information to all caregivers, regardless of the language they use Sends the message to caregivers that the classroom community is inclusive	Provides resources to caregivers in the languages they use.

Find a blank form online at scholastic.com/RootedResources.

Here we offer starting points for weaving students' home practices into the classroom environment. Many of them may seem familiar but are likely only in English, making multilingual students and their families feel invisible.

- Ask families to send in boxes for food items they typically buy, including boxes in a variety of languages. Create a chart with the empty boxes and labels gathered and read them with the children. Help them see that opportunities for reading exist everywhere.

Cindy Quiroz designs her classroom door using images from social media to reflect her students' 21st century language and social practices.

- Go to the supermarket and take photos of product labels, including labels in languages other than English. Then examine the photos with your students.

- Take a walk around the neighborhood with students and read and photograph the signs. Notice in which languages the signs are written. Talk about the purposes these signs have.

- Make or have children make signs for important places around the school building, such as the office, the bathrooms, and the gym. Then, with the children, post the signs in the appropriate locations.

- Explore students' names as a wonderful way to personalize the language ecology of a classroom. Students may create self-portraits or family portraits that they label with names. Their names might be part of a highly visible attendance chart or job chart. By studying the spelling of letters of their own names, their classmates' names, or the names of people important to them, children learn the characteristics of each letter and how to use all letters in a word to read it, not just the first letter. Also, focus on the pronunciation of each name and how the letter sounds vary, depending on the language in which you're speaking.

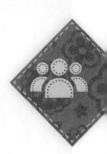

Into the Classroom

Exploring Children's Names

It is the beginning of the school year in Karina's second-grade bilingual class. Karina is working on establishing a classroom community and is asking the children to share family stories about the origins of their names. Because children's names are so central to their identities and connect them deeply to their families, learning about names is a powerful way to support young readers and should be where early literacy begins. In a commitment to involve families, she sends home the letter on the next page in Spanish and English.

In the next few days, children share their name stories with the class during morning meeting. They prepare by writing their stories and creating illustrations. Then their work is posted in a display in the hall outside the classroom. Here are some other possible engagements related to children's names.

- Read name-related books to the class. Note also that several of these are available in English and in Spanish. (See some suggestions on page 60.)
- Ask parents to write down in their preferred language the story of their children's names. Then have children share with their classmates how they got their names.

- If your students are young, label their cubbies with their name next to their picture. From a literacy perspective, you may want to explore how to write a name in other languages— for example, José, Joseph, Josef, and Ioseph.

- Before class, write children's names on cards and place the cards on a table near the door. When children enter, have them choose their name cards. Then ask them to compare their names with those of classmates. (Often, they will notice just the first letter, so encourage them to go further with spelling.) Have them say their names to one another, using the pronunciation their families prefer. This name-sharing practice builds awareness of particular letter sounds or accented syllables.

- Sing a song that includes the children's names. Be sure to pronounce each child's name according to the family's preference.

Dear Caregiver,

Our school year has started, and we are rapidly getting acquainted with one another. When children know each other's stories, the learning environment is richer. I always start the year with a study of our names—specifically, the origins of our names. I ask you to talk with your child and, together, write the story of his or her name, using these questions that we developed as a class:

- What does my name mean?
- Am I named after someone? If so, whom?
- Why did you select this name for me?

You might share the meaning of your child's name or something about the person after whom he or she is named. It is important that you both talk and write.

When children study their names, it empowers them, gives them a sense of belonging, and offers glimpses into their family history.

I will be sharing the story of my name, too, and reading books that focus on names, such as...

- *Alma and How She Got Her Name* (2018) by Juana Martínez-Neal

- *The Name Jar* (2001) by Yangsook Choi

- *Chrysanthemum* (1991) by Kevin Henkes

- *My Name Is Yoon* (2014) by Helen Recorvits

- *Your Name Is a Song* (2020) by Jamilah Thompkins-Bigelow

- *Thunder Boy Jr.* (2016) by Sherman Alexie

- *My Name Is Jorge: On Both Sides of the River* (1999) by Jane Medina.

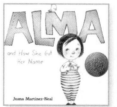

Thank you in advance for taking the time to do this homework with your child.

Su maestra,
Karina

Teaching Concepts of Print With Predictable Books

It's important for young emergent bilingual children to acquire the basic concepts of print, as well as knowledge of the alphabet and letter-sound correspondence. From our perspective, the issue at hand is how to create opportunities for them to build their reading identities, while capitalizing on their entire linguistic repertoire, which includes developing their concepts of print.

Sometimes, early literacy experiences begin with isolated bits of language. For example, when students are learning to read in Spanish, teachers often begin with syllables: "*ma, me, mi, mo, mu.*" They then move to studying words, and then sentences. Finally, they move to reading simple stories. However, those experiences offer children vocabulary that is too controlled, often at the expense of making meaning and experiencing relevance.

Instead, we propose that you read aloud quality predictable books, which allow children to join in on the reading because of their naturally repetitive patterns. Children can predict what comes next because the text flows naturally. The power of a good predictable book is that it carries the reader. It invites him or her to make connections to prior knowledge. Captivating predictable books offer children access to the richness of language and craft. And they're available in English, other languages, and bilingual versions.

What a Good Predictable Book Offers the Emergent Bilingual Reader

- Illustrations that support and extend the text
- Natural language (how people talk and use language in a particular community)
- Repetitive, yet meaningful text throughout: phrases, sentences, repeating words
- Rhythmic language
- Ideas that build on one another (cumulative text)
- Familiar topics
- Stories that capture oral traditions, poetry, and song (culturally sustaining texts)
- Familiar characters, when the books are part of a series

Given the wide variety of predictable books available, you can carefully and intentionally select them. Choose based on your knowledge of emergent bilingual children, their needs as readers, and their knowledge of predictable

books. For example, when reading the bilingual predictable book, *Maria Had a Little Llama/María tenía una llamita* by Angela Dominguez (2013), you can begin by showing children the cover and inviting them to describe what they notice. After a few comments, ask the children to predict what the book might be about.

Consider translanguaging and remind children that they can share their thoughts using their entire linguistic repertoire. For example, nudge them to notice key details about the cover and make predictions about the book in the language of their choice. Read the book's title and author and illustrator's names while pointing to them. As you read, demonstrate directionality. For example, in English and Spanish, readers read left to right, top to bottom. In other languages, such as Arabic, Hebrew, Urdu, and Persian, directionality in reading is right to left. Explain that you will read the book to them and stop at spots to ask them to predict what will happen next, again in the language of their choice. Doing this allows them to capitalize on their linguistic repertoires to construct meaning. While reading the book, share the meanings of challenging words by pointing to them, providing synonyms, and/or asking someone to translate their meaning. This is also an opportunity to discuss the purpose of punctuation and capitalization and to guide them in developing knowledge of letters.

When you've finished the book, spend a few minutes talking about it. Questions such as "What did you like about this book?" and "What did you notice about its language?" provide opportunities for children to draw upon their entire linguistic repertoire, making the discussion richer. Lastly, offer the book to children so they can explore it on their own during independent reading time. In a follow-up reading of the book, ask emergent bilingual children to join you. Encourage them to make predictions. Maybe cover a repetitive phrase that challenges the emergent bilingual children to enhance their abilities to predict.

You may also want to revisit the book on another day and focus on the semantic cueing system (what makes sense) or the graphophonic cueing system (what looks and sounds correct). For example, if you want emergent bilingual children to pay attention to the semantic cueing system, choose a word or phrase from the book, cover it, and ask children to think about a word or phrase that would make sense. The last step would then be to cover the word or phrase and talk with the children to confirm whether their prediction makes sense (synonym) or it matches the actual text. It is important that you discuss with them why the prediction made sense or if it changed the meaning.

If you're going to focus on the graphophonic cueing system, choose a predictable book that provides emergent bilingual children with semantic and syntactic support. Choose a word from the book and cover the end of it. Ask the child to predict what the word might be, given the letter or letters he or she can see. Slowly reveal more letters until the child is able to determine the words. You can also help the child learn the sound of individual letters and chunks and/or patterns by connecting the target word to words that they already know.

Another option to help the children pay attention to all three cueing systems is to write the text of the predictable book on sentence strips, and ask the emergent bilingual child to organize the sentence strips in a way that makes sense, at first with some support of the illustrations, then slowly removing the scaffold. It is important to allow children to use their entire linguistic repertoires for all of these activities.

Student-Made Predictable Books

Children can also be authors by composing a predictable book that integrates the languages they speak. This is a great opportunity for students to discuss from a writer's perspective concepts of print (title, author, illustrator, etc.). They can talk about spaces on the page for drawing and spaces for writing. From there, you might want to have each child compose a page. When the book is completed, the class can celebrate its publication with a read-aloud.

Emergent bilingual children need ample opportunities to return to a favorite predictable book over and over. Sometimes they might do a choral reading of the book, sometimes they might read it with a partner, and sometimes they may read it independently. These practices go a long way in helping emergent bilingual children develop a positive stance toward reading.

Santiago is in first grade. He speaks Spanish and English at home. He wrote this predictable book in English.

Teaching Phonemic Awareness and Phonics in Context

Phonemic awareness and phonics are essential to developing readers, as long as these are not taught in isolation. Phonemic awareness is an understanding that spoken words are composed of individual sounds called phonemes. Phonics focuses on the understanding of letter (grapheme)-sound (phoneme) relationships and their spelling. When taught in context, both skills help students decode words and, over time, read more complex texts independently. Moreover, phonemic awareness and phonics, while often considered foundational, should not be taught in isolation and solely as a precursor to reading (Shanahan, 2020). Reading development is not strictly linear but is best described as a dynamic process and for emergent bilinguals, necessarily involves their linguistic repertoire.

When tackling phonemic awareness and phonics with emergent bilinguals, it is important to value the language they use most often at home, which can be difficult because so many programs target foundational skills solely in English. However, when teaching in a dual-language bilingual program, phonemic awareness should be covered in both English and in relevant ways in the students' home languages. For example, examine rhyming words in the home language. When teaching in a monolingual program, you can invite the children to engage their families in sharing songs and spending time exploring the rhyming sounds and comparing them to rhyming sounds in English. We feel strongly that for striving emergent bilingual readers, or those taking longer than others to learn to read, teachers must provide opportunities for them to receive multimodal foundational support in the languages they speak. Otherwise, they will be denied intervention in their languages and, by default, be tracked into English-only approaches.

For emergent bilingual students, the teaching of phonics and phonemic awareness needs to be contextualized in reading authentic texts. Phonics in isolation becomes an impossible task in a language the child is learning. To teach phonics well, it is important to know individual children as readers and understand their needs. Some children need more explicit phonics instruction (always in context and with the intention that reading for meaning is the goal), while others develop understandings about phonics with more ease. Traditionally, phonics instruction has been carried out through innumerable drills and worksheets that have students isolate sounds. Students spend so much time learning the sounds in individual words, they never get to the task of reading. Consequently, they become disengaged because they never see how phonics can actually help them with their reading. Furthermore, those drills and worksheets are usually in English and divorced from authentic meaning.

Even English-speaking students may be stumped by what they are supposed to do! My son (Laura's) was recently sorting pictures containing images that began with either *n* or *p*, to help him learn letter sounds. After looking at a picture of a nest with eggs, he declared, "This one's a mystery!", because he was focusing on the eggs in the picture and not the nest. While my son has a wide English vocabulary, many emergent bilinguals are just in the process of acquiring it and, therefore, nearly every picture clue may be a "mystery" for them. Phonemic awareness and phonics instruction for emergent bilinguals makes sense when their interests, intentions, and own words are taken into consideration. They need to be immersed in analyzing phonics, using words that matter to them and taught in context.

At the core of reading is the construction of meaning. Without question, children need decoding skills to comprehend text and transact with it. However, too often, emergent bilinguals are expected to learn to decode before having any meaningful experiences with text, which deprives them of the enjoyment of reading. When teaching phonics, we must always keep in mind a vision of the kind of readers we want to help develop: readers who know that reading is the construction of meaning, readers who understand that sounding out is only one of many word-solving strategies, and readers who are active, engaged, and in conversations with themselves, the text, the author, other texts, and so forth. The teaching of phonics should never be in question. However, *how we teach it* to emergent bilinguals must be rooted in their multilingual resources.

Children's Writing, Phonics, and Phonemic Awareness

Learning to read and learning to write are tightly interconnected. When children are encouraged to sound out words as they write them and use invented (phonetic) spelling, and are given appropriate support, guidance, and demonstrations, they develop awareness of the alphabetic system. For example, a child might at first hear only the letter *l* in *love*. But when the teacher helps him or her stretch the word ("l-o-v-v-e"), the child will likely first hear the *v*. In time, the child will also hear the *o* and be able to write *lov*. When children use invented spelling to convey messages, they develop metalinguistic awareness. They might compare the spelling of words that follow similar patterns and discover that only one letter sets them apart: *cake, bake*. Invented spelling also helps children develop curiosity about language, letter-sound correspondence, word patterns, etc.

In essence, when children use phonetic spelling, they are applying their evolving knowledge of letters and phonemes. Watching them write and reading their writing enables us to find out about their knowledge of the alphabetic system and their phonics and phonemic awareness skills, and, from there, provide explicit instruction more effectively. Children need opportunities to explore letter-sound relationships on their own terms and receive explicit instruction. Invented spelling is never static. As children become more sophisticated spellers, their knowledge of phonics and phonemic awareness also develops further.

When young children write, capitalizing on their entire linguistic repertoire using invented spelling, they are using everything they know to create their own meaningful texts. It is possible that letter-sound correspondence from one named language will appear in the spelling of another named language. For example, a child might hear "dejrsispriti" when trying to write "The horse is pretty." What is important at this point is that the teacher works within what Lev Vygotsky named as the child's Zone of Proximal Development (ZPD) (Vygotsky, 1978), that space where the teacher can support the child in gaining deeper, more complex understandings about print. What matters is focusing first on the meaning, the child's written message—what he or she is attempting to tell the reader. Next, ask a question such as "What color is the horse?" Then point to the words *the* and *horse*, and sound them out slowly, helping the child to make each letter-sound correspondence by sounding out individual words and really stretching each sound. You might also point to the word *the* and remind the child that it is one of the class's sight words, and that in English the letter *h* sometimes sounds like a *j* in Spanish. Depending on what you know about the child, those two points might be all you work on. On another day, you might work with the child on the letter-sound correspondence of a word such as *pretty*.

When young children write, capitalizing on their entire linguistic repertoire using invented spelling, they are using everything they know to create their own meaningful texts. It is possible that letter-sound correspondence from one named language will appear in the spelling of another named language.

For the most part, letter-sound correspondence in Spanish is very predictable—that is, each letter has for the most part one sound. As mentioned previously, in Spanish, the teaching of writing and reading has often started with teaching syllables (e.g., *ma, me, mi, mo, mu*). Then, students are asked to put these syllables together (e.g., Mi mamá me mima [My mother cares for me]). This often results in a sentence filled with controlled vocabulary. We recommend that when reading in Spanish, teachers help children examine the syllables of a word within the context of authentic reading or writing experiences. For example, begin by reading the poem to the class. Then identify a key word, write it separately, break it down into syllables, examine each syllable, helping the child stretch the word to hear the different sounds that make up the word. Then read the word together with the child. Afterward, it is important to go back to reading the whole text together one more time. It is important to help them see that the purpose of these experiences is not doing exercises in isolation, but reading a text that make sense.

When working with a child's writing, identify one word from the child's writing, spell it conventionally, and if you want to study with the child how it is composed, break it down into syllables. Assist the child in hearing and sounding out each syllable. Then go back to the child's writing. Focus on the message the child is conveying and accept approximations. In spite of the predictability of letter-sound correspondence in Spanish, give children the opportunities to read predictable texts, songs, and poems, and to explore letter-sound correspondence (syllables) in the context of predictable books. Help them also develop their ability to hear syllables in the context of their own writing. Often, children will hear the vowels first because vowels tend to have a stronger sound in Spanish than English (Hudelson, 1981). For example, a child may write in Spanish: Ooaia/Yo quiero a mi mamá. In English, it would be: Ilvmom/I love my mom.

Closing Thoughts

The reading process is complex. A translanguaging vision of reading posits that reading starts with the person. In other words, the multilingual person does not read in one language or the other, but rather brings his or her whole linguistic repertoire and social repertoire to the text. Reading cuts across named languages, modalities, and experiences. That's why we insist that you encourage emergent bilingual children to read books in their home language, the language they're learning, and with features from different linguistic repertoires. We also encourage you to make sure they know themselves as readers who have particular interests and areas of expertise. As teachers, we want children to recognize that reading is a meaningful act and engage them in reading as it exists in their communities.

Suggestions for Professional Development

The professional development suggestions in this chapter guide you to examine your own experiences as a reader (and writer). We also ask you to explore your collection of predictable books and to tap into the potential of nursery rhymes, songs, and chants as you more intentionally and purposefully plan for translanguaging in early literacy experiences.

As you become more knowledgeable about the reading process, it is important that you examine how you learned to read and write. In Appendix B, we offer you a recollection with some questions that can lead you to examine your own experiences as a reader and a writer.

1 Analyze with a colleague predictable books in your classroom and ways to incorporate opportunities for translanguaging. After looking through your library, take out a few books that you identify as predictable books. (Review our description of what characterizes a predictable book.) What makes each book predictable? Would all the students in your class understand the patterns? If not, what could you do to support them to understand what makes the book predictable? Does the book have controlled vocabulary? How can you tell? With a partner, read through three to five of these books. Think about what you could do to support students in understanding the patterns that make each book predictable. Also think about how you could incorporate students' language and social resources to understand the book.

2 Create resources for the children to learn from each other's cultural and linguistic backgrounds by incorporating family input. Ask the parents/guardians in your class to share via video, audio, or in person a nursery rhyme from their cultural background. Ask the parents to provide the oral version as well as the print version. Introduce it to the class. You can create a class book, a center, or a poster with these nursery rhymes.

3 Pick a nursery rhyme that you know well and analyze it. Who are the characters? Which language features would you like to highlight, including the nursery rhyme's phonemic awareness development possibilities? Find ways to make connections between the nursery rhyme and your students' lives and interests, if possible. Create a plan to teach it to the class, including introducing it, reciting it, and pointing out features. Introduce the nursery rhyme to the class and support the home-school connection by sending resources for families home so that children can share it with someone they live with.

CHAPTER 4

Supporting Emergent Bilinguals Through Shared Reading and Guided Reading

"We need to offer children 'surround sound' reading. We need to give them the time and space to read like a super reader every day of the week, every week of the month, every month of the year, in school and out of school."

—PAM ALLYN AND ERNEST MORRELL

Both shared reading and guided reading are components of balanced literacy. Ideally, they work together to provide students with the resources they need to engage in sustained independent reading of self-selected texts (Burkins & Yaris, 2016). Shared reading, guided reading, and independent reading position students as active constructors in their development as readers (Fountas & Pinnell, 2016; Stephens, Harste, & Clyde, 2019). In this chapter, we re-envision shared reading and guided reading from the perspective of the emergent bilingual student and offer you a translanguaging vision for both.

Shared Reading: Vision and Possibilities

When I (Laura) was a beginning teacher, I learned to define shared reading as joyful time for productive learning about books and print, and that joy was a driving force behind students' reading engagement and learning. Although shared reading is most commonly taught in grades K–2, it can—and should—be done throughout elementary school and beyond.

Shared reading is a literacy event in which a group of children participate actively in the reading of a text, with the guidance of a more experienced reader (the teacher).

Shared reading is a literacy event in which a group of children participate actively in the reading of a text, with the guidance of a more experienced reader (the teacher). To prepare for shared reading, select a text that the children will enjoy and that will push them forward, together, in the reading process. Because students are actively participating in the reading, regardless of the grade, the teacher should offer an enlarged version of the text that all students can clearly see, such as a big book, a poem, or a morning message transcribed on chart paper or displayed on a smartboard. It is possible also to give older students copies of the text. Usually the teacher selects a text (or a section of a text) that is a bit challenging for the children. During the reading, she may model for students how to read with expression and cadence, how to think aloud about a particular situation or a point the author is making, and how to enjoy the reading—and get the most out of it. Teachers also often use shared reading to discuss concepts of print (e.g., point out text elements such as title, author, illustrator; demonstrate that English is read from left to right, top to bottom) as well as punctuation, capitalization, and letter-sound correspondence. The teacher can support the children by reading alphabet books. For older students, the teacher can shift the focus to modeling the use of reading strategies, punctuation, a particular aspect of a genre, or an author's craft. Shared reading offers children the communal experience of learning alongside others and always should lead to a discussion of the text.

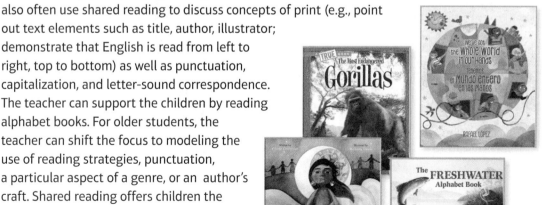

A Translanguaging Perspective on Shared Reading

When teachers use translanguaging during shared reading, they demonstrate how to approach text as a reader, using their entire linguistic repertoire. For example, if the teacher is bilingual, she could show how she approaches the reading using both languages. If the teacher is not bilingual, she can still make space for students' translanguaging during the reading. One starting point is to select a text that is culturally and linguistically sustaining,

such as a poem in *Yes! We Are Latinos: Poems and Prose About the Latino Experience* by Alma Flor Ada and Isabel Campoy (2016). In addition to selecting poems that allow children to experience bilingual authors, the teacher can also create opportunities for children to share their insights with the entire class or with a partner, making sure that they can "bring their whole selves" and language resources to the reading (García, 2020). The teacher might invite students to respond in any language and through multiple modalities. She might use cognates to help the children think about different word meanings. If the teacher does not speak the children's home language, she can ask children who do to use their entire linguistic repertoire to communicate with others in the class.

Strategies You Can Demonstrate in Shared Reading

Plan each shared reading intentionally, in ways that ensure emergent bilingual children will be able to engage in the reading using all their resources. Your instruction during shared reading should be based on your observations and knowledge of the children, as well as your knowledge of the reading process. You may decide that you want to use a poem, and at other times you might select an excerpt of a fiction or nonfiction book. By the end of their time in your class, children should be familiar with many reading strategies that they can use when they read independently. Here are some specific strategies that embrace translanguaging that you can teach in shared reading:

- Demonstrate how, in many languages, readers read from left to right, whereas in others, such as Arabic, Urdu, and Hebrew, they read from right to left.

- Draw on prior knowledge: Ask the children to ask themselves, "What do I know about this topic?" Create an open invitation for students to share their knowledge multimodally and through their language resources.

- Preview the book. Look at pages of the book from beginning to end. What is familiar and what is not?

- Look carefully at the cover and predict what the book might be about. Consider whether students have the prior knowledge necessary to make accurate predictions.

- Read a paragraph and visualize what it's about, either orally or through drawing. Share your visualization with a partner. Then invite the children to do the same, using all of their languages to explain and deepen their visualization.

- Tap into students' visual literacy. As you read the book with students, use its pictures as additional meaning-making clues and allow students to talk about the pictures using any language resources available to them.

- Show students how you self-monitor as you read by asking yourself, "Did what I just read make sense?" Model this, if possible, in the students' language other than English, so they know they can make meaning using all of their language resources. If you don't speak a student's language, you can let that student know that he or she can use his or her linguistic repertoire to make sense of the book.

A Day at the Park

On a beautiful sunny day, Mrs. C and Mrs. P were at the park when they saw a blue bird. Mrs. P pointed and said, "yo veo un pajarito azul." Mrs. C heard the bird and said, "She chirps so loudly." As they pet the blue jay, the feathers felt soft and gentle. The fresh smell reminded Mrs. C of her pet parakeet.

Second-grade teachers create a text with translanguaging for shared reading.

- Explore the many ways to predict. Encourage students to ask themselves, "What word would make sense here?". They can also stop at a certain point and make a prediction about the story. As students predict, be sure they tap into their entire linguistic repertoire.

- Confirm, disconfirm, and self-correct. The teacher can remind students that this process can happen while capitalizing on their entire linguistic repertoire.

- Break a word into parts. Is there a word within the word? Sound it out. Students who speak more than one language can also ask themselves, "Does this word remind me of any word I know in my other language?" (This works especially well with languages like Spanish, Italian, French, and Romanian. It also works with cognates, which are words that have similar spelling and meaning across named languages.)

- Make inferences about the story, given what you already know about it. Invite the children to make inferences, using all their linguistic and social resources.

- Reread a part that confused you, and then say it back to yourself in any language you may speak.

- Monitor comprehension: Ask questions about what is happening in the text in any language.

- Take notes in your own words, in any language that helps students to process the information.

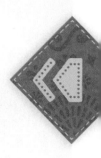

Action 6

Use the Burke Reading Interview to Learn the Theories of Emergent Bilingual Readers

Not only do we teachers hold beliefs about reading and ourselves as readers, but so do our students, including our emergent bilingual students. Those beliefs guide the reading strategies they use.

In this action, we discuss the Burke Reading Interview by Goodman, Watson, and Burke (1987), which helps you explore with students what reading is, what makes a good reader, and what strategies good readers use. It was designed with the monolingual reader in mind, so we have adapted it for the emergent bilingual reader.

Select an emergent bilingual child from your class and ask the child the following questions adapted from the Burke Reading Interview.

1. When you are reading and come to something you don't know, what do you do? (Children may refer to a language other than English, such as, "I look for a word that is similar in Spanish.")

2. Do you ever do anything else? Which language resources do you use to figure out the word you don't know?

3. What does it mean to you to be a bilingual reader?

4. Who is a good bilingual reader you know? What makes [name] a good bilingual reader?

5. Do you think [name] ever comes to a word or phrase he or she doesn't know?

   - If yes, what do you think he or she does?

   - If no, what do you think he or she should do?

6. If you know a bilingual reader is having trouble reading, how would you help him or her? What would your teacher do to help that reader?

7. How did you learn to read in two languages?

8. What would you like to do better as a bilingual reader?

9. Do you think you're a good bilingual reader? Why or why not?

10. What do you think you could do to be a better reader?

11. Do you think it's important to read in more than one language? Why?

Record and study students' responses and check whether they are capitalizing on their entire linguistic repertoires and social resources. Use this information to create mini-lessons that will nudge them to use their bilingualism to construct deeper meanings as they read.

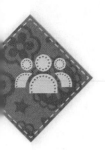

What Does Translanguaging in Shared Reading Look Like?

Let's look inside Karina's second-grade classroom to get a sense of how one teacher puts some of these ideas together for her emergent bilinguals: four who speak Spanish and three who speak Albanian. Karina starts the shared reading experience by displaying the book on the board: *Guacamole: Un poema para cocinar/A Cooking Poem* written by Jorge Argueta (2016) and illustrated by Margarita Sada, which is presented in Spanish and English. She begins by reading aloud an excerpt from the poem in English and referring to parts of it in Spanish, asking children to follow along. Karina points to each word, thinking aloud as she reads. She asks, "I wonder what the word *delicious* means."

Let me reread the previous sentence to see if I can figure it out." She talks about the meaning of *delicious* after rereading the text, and then continues reading. Later in the reading, she points to the word *avocados* and the picture of the avocado. She asks a child to say the word in Spanish. "Aguacate," he replies. She adds *avocado* and *aguacate* to a chart and draws a picture of an avocado next to them. Then she goes back to the book and points to the illustration of the avocado. She reminds the children that when they're reading and unsure about a word, they can look at the picture and also think about the word in English and/or Spanish.

When she's finished reading, she asks the children for their thoughts and ideas about the poem. In their responses, the children are invited to use their entire linguistic repertoires. (Each child is sitting next to someone who shares his or her language repertoire to facilitate communication.) Karina has also taken the time to ask parents for the meanings of some words in the language(s) children speak with family members, so that she can create a chart to facilitate student conversation. She has a chart with the words from the poem written in English, Spanish, and Albanian and goes over those words with the children. When appropriate, she asks them to

Para hacer un sabroso guacamole
que deje a tu mamá, a tu papá
y a tus hermanitos
pidiendo más,
necesitas
cuatro aguacates grandes
como piedras verdes,
dos limones frescos
grandes y brillosos
como canicas de cristal.
Necesitas unas hojitas de cilantro
verdes como un ramito de tréboles.
Necesitas sal
y nada más.

❊

To make a delicious guacamole
that will leave your mother and father
and your little brother and sister
begging for more,
you need
four big avocados,
like green precious stones,
and two fresh limes,
big shiny ones,
round as crystal marbles.
You need some cilantro leaves,
green as a four-leaf clover,
you need salt
and that's all.

dramatize the word or use gestures to think about its meaning. When necessary, they use a digital translation tool.

At the end of the shared reading session, Karina asks all students to dramatize the poem, pairing students strategically. She might, for example, pair a more outgoing child with a less outgoing child, or pair children by language.

The following day, Karina reads the poem to the children. Then she asks them, as they close their eyes, to think about the images the words conjure in their minds. When she's finished, she asks the children open-ended questions that lead them to share any connections they can make about the text. She points to the chart of questions posted in the classroom, which have been translated into Spanish and Albanian, and reminds them that they can share using their entire linguistic repertoire. Through the questions that she asks, her students enter into the conversation. "What images did you have in your mind as you read the poem? What personal connections did you make to the poem? Are there words you think are interesting?"

The next day, the class reads the poem chorally once. Karina then splits the class into two groups. She tells Group 1 that they will read the lines that have the number 1 next to them, and Group 2 that they will read the lines that are marked number 2. The two groups then practice reading their respective lines a few times. This practice of choral reading is important because it provides students with a different experience of reading the same text. You can create new ways of grouping students as they get to know the poem.

Next, she tells the children they will be learning a strategy that will help them become more independent readers: figuring out what to do when they come to a word they don't know. She displays the poem again, but this time she places a sticky note over some key words. The children then ask themselves what word would make sense in those positions, including words they know in other named languages. Karina reminds them that when readers read for meaning, they substitute an unknown word with one that makes sense. Karina writes the words children say, even if they are in a language other than English, on the sticky notes and invites the children to reread the text. The children and Karina discuss which words make sense before uncovering the word.

On the last day, Karina tells the students that they will be reading the poem for homework. She also asks them to practice the strategies they have learned, such as what to do when they come to a word they don't know.

Because this shared reading experience was stretched over days, Karina provided her students with multiple opportunities to engage with text, while drawing upon their linguistic and social resources. By using students' resources as a starting point, she could ensure that students in her class could engage personally with the text.

Guided Reading: Vision and Possibilities

In Rebecca's second-grade dual-language bilingual classroom, the reading mini-lesson has just ended, and independent reading is starting. Some students are at desks, and some are on cushions in the reading nook. As soon as her students are settled in, Rebecca calls the names of four children, based on knowledge she has about them as readers from conferencing with them during independent reading time. They are excited; they love being in a small group with their teacher. Guided reading offers teachers and students the possibility of interacting with one another in a small-group setting, while working on specific reading skills and strategies to usher students along the reading process. It is generally considered the primary engine driving students' reading progress across elementary schools.

Small-group instruction, such as guided reading, is a powerful way to support emergent bilingual readers.

Teachers group students intentionally, strategically, and temporarily, based on students' needs. Using their knowledge of the students' reading, teachers assemble a group of children who would benefit from instruction in a particular strategy (preview a book, figure out unfamiliar words, make predictions, preview a nonfiction text, etc.). They select a book or text that offers students multiple opportunities to work on the strategy. They model the strategy, provide explicit guidance, and then listen as students try out the strategy. With proper scaffolding, students can then apply the strategy as they read the text by themselves. Just like a parent who is teaching a child to ride a bike, the teacher takes in information about how the child is navigating the strategy and provides support toward independence.

Typically, students are grouped by the text level at which they're reading, rather than by strategies, strength, or areas of challenge. Yet, Irene Fountas and Gay Su Pinnell warn us that reading levels were not intended to group students nor should we consider guided reading as a *fixed set of procedures* constituting a silver bullet (2012). They remind us that the goal is for students to become strategic, efficient, effective readers and therefore the responsive quality of instruction during guided reading is critical.

The reality of guided reading for emergent bilinguals is complex because they are learning about reading and language simultaneously. While some researchers have pointed out ways that the guided reading process can be tweaked to aid emergent bilinguals, those modifications are simply add-ons to the process and do not address students' bilingualism (Ascenzi-Moreno & Quiñones, 2020). From a translanguaging perspective, it is important to ask how students' bilingualism can play a central role in reading and how it can be an asset during guided reading.

Guided reading offers teachers and students the possibility of interacting with one another in a small-group setting, while working on specific reading skills and strategies to usher students along the reading process.

Consider these two scenarios: In one guided reading lesson, the teacher adds onto the lesson by introducing and teaching students several vocabulary words that students will encounter in the book. In another guided reading lesson, students talk about how when they read in Spanish, they identify syllables and blend them. Then the teacher connects that observation to how readers of English typically look for word chunks. In the first lesson, the teacher is solely front-loading vocabulary, a technique that teachers employ in monolingual classrooms that is useful but lengthens the lesson. In the second lesson, the teacher recognizes that the students will engage in the lesson as bilingual people and uses their knowledge of reading across languages to support and guide them as they read (Ascenzi-Moreno & Quiñones, 2020).

From a translanguaging perspective, emergent bilinguals are seen as resourceful and competent users of a unified linguistic and social repertoire. They are developing as readers in general, as well as managing the intricacies and specificity of what reading looks like in particular named languages. We propose moving away from a standardized monolingual structure for guided reading, where modifications for emergent bilinguals are added on, to one that truly engages students' bilingualism (Ascenzi-Moreno & Quiñones, 2020). The following research and anecdotes presented about guided reading are the result of collaborative research between a bilingual teacher educator and bilingual teacher researcher (Ascenzi-Moreno & Quiñones, 2020).

Into the Classroom

What Does Translanguaging in Guided Reading Look Like?

Rebecca has called a group of Spanish-speaking emergent bilinguals to the rug for a guided reading lesson in Spanish. The students are reading a text about worms. In thinking about selecting this text, Rebecca knows that the students need to strengthen their ability to figure out the meaning of unknown words when they are reading about topics that may not be so familiar. She decides to carry out this lesson in Spanish so that she can leverage her students' knowledge in the lesson. She knows that once the students are comfortable applying the strategy in Spanish, they will be able to generalize the skill to all their reading performances, with support.

There is some tricky language in the book. For example, the author uses *cavar* for *dig*, when many Spanish-speaking students would use the phrase *sacar tierra* or the word *excavar*. The students discuss ways they would say *dig* in Spanish, along with the word in the book. Rebecca shows students ways to figure out what words mean by looking at the pictures, or by thinking about words they know in Spanish that are similar, such as *excavar*. From there, Rebecca listens in as students read and figure out the meaning of words such as *colocar* (to place) and *lombrices de tierra* (earthworms). At the end of the lesson, she leads a short discussion about what worms do and then urges students to read the book again in school and at home and talk to their parents about some of the words in the book, as well as the ideas in the book.

Rebecca creates a chart in Spanish with questions to support students to figure out vocabulary. [Translation: What does it mean? When you don't know what it means ... look at the picture. Look at the words around it and think... what could it mean?]

Creating the Guided Reading Group

Usually, the teacher selects students who need to work on a particular reading strategy. When working with emerging bilingual students, though, she needs to consider when it would be advantageous to group students who have similar linguistic backgrounds and when would it be advantageous to group those who have different ones. In addition to thinking about linguistic background, she needs to take into account the students' socio-culturally-based prior knowledge and decide if it would be beneficial to use that information to assemble a group. For example, she may want to group students who have knowledge about decoding through their understanding of Spanish and build off this knowledge.

Selecting a Text

Choosing the right text is always complex because it must present some challenges, but not so many that the teaching point becomes muddled, and students are left frustrated. For emergent bilinguals, text selection raises unique questions. For example, do students have the background knowledge about information in the text? How can the teacher help the students connect their background knowledge to the text's content?

It is also important to determine whether the text is original or a translation. Translations from English to Spanish can be tricky, especially when simple words in English translate to long, complex words in Spanish. For example, the word *bat* is a simple CVC word (consonant, vowel, consonant) and, therefore, easily decodable for most emergent readers. However, *bat* translates to *murciélago* in Spanish—a word that would be too complex for most young readers because of its four syllables and a diphthong.

In addition, it is important to analyze texts in any language for language variety. For example, like English, Spanish is spoken a bit differently from region to region. People from the Dominican Republic, Ecuador, Mexico, and Argentina, while all speaking Spanish, may have different names for one object, such as a backpack or a kite. It is also possible that within one country there are different names for the particular object. This should be considered when selecting texts for guided reading, because the words they contain, while being in the language the children speak, may not be ones the children in your classroom are familiar with.

Teaching the Lesson

Consider the following contrast: In a typical monolingual guided reading lesson, the teacher isolates a strategy, such as making inferences, and asks the students in one language to make inferences in the same language. In a translanguaged guided reading lesson, the teacher may ask the students to start making inferences using any of their language resources and then move to the language the book is in. By doing that, she provides students with a pathway to access their general knowledge about reading. She sends a message that the thinking work students do while reading *is reading*, regardless of the language they do it in.

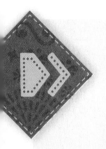

Action 7

Create Introductions to Guided Reading Lessons for Emergent Bilingual Students

In this action, we show you how to create an introduction to a guided reading lesson that invites and brings forth students' bilingualism. Once you select a text, think about the central concepts it contains. For example, is the book about farm animals, or different kinds of eggs, or making a puppet, or going on a nature walk? Don't think about only the reading strategy you want to teach (e.g., vowel combinations, vocabulary, semantic cues, cloze procedure). That said, it is critical to keep comprehension at the center. Let's say I chose a book on rice. Before introducing the strategy to students, I would ask them how they say *rice* at home, how they prepare rice, and in what ways they eat it. By doing that, I set the stage for students to engage in the reading by bringing their resources to the forefront. Start by asking yourself what words are associated with the topic. Consider pictures, objects, and actions you can share with students to awaken their interest, prior knowledge, and authentic drive to communicate with you and their peers. During the lesson, allow students to talk to each other in whatever language(s) they feel comfortable using. Ask them to think about their personal connections to the text's topic.

Listening to Students

A skilled teacher listens to students read with the three cueing systems described earlier in mind. As students read, she might listen for their fluency but also for miscues, or errors, and determine if those miscues are due to lapses or gaps in the use of the visual, syntactic, or semantic cueing system. But for emergent bilingual students, teachers need to be attuned to how students' linguistic resources and their bilingual identities support them as readers.

There is a solid body of research that acknowledges that emergent bilinguals will make miscues related to being language learners (Ascenzi-Moreno, 2018; Briceño & Klein, 2018; K. Goodman & Y. Goodman, 2014). Teachers must listen to students as they read, with an eye to language. In what ways does students' bilingualism impact their reading? Are they making any kinds of language-specific miscues? What am I learning about my students as bilingual readers?

Ending the Lesson

A guided reading lesson usually ends with a discussion of the text. The teacher typically reminds students of the importance of using the strategy they studied and practiced whenever they read. This sends a message that, in every reading experience, students should be reading effectively and efficiently. Because the focus should be on understanding and connecting to the themes in a text, it's important to invite students to participate using their entire linguistic repertoire. Think about how they are using their bilingual "powers" as a source for reading.

Closing Thoughts

In this chapter, we demonstrated how two pillars of balanced literacy can be reconceptualized to meet the needs of emergent bilinguals. Both shared reading and guided reading are powerful tools in supporting students as readers. However, they have been traditionally conceptualized from a monolingual perspective. Reimagining how shared and guided reading can be actualized when students' multilingualism is central to reading instruction and the norm is key to supporting emergent bilinguals' reading development.

Suggestions for Professional Development

1 Bring to a grade-level meeting two or three completed Burke Reading Interviews from emergent bilingual children in your class, and review them with your grade-level colleagues. What patterns do you notice? What surprises you? What do you learn about these particular children as readers? What mini-lessons and conversations about reading might you have, based on information in these Burke Reading Interviews? What changes could you make as a grade-level team, based on what you learn from the Burke Reading Interviews to ensure sensitivity to multilingualism as the norm in your class?

2 Review the section on shared reading in this chapter and prepare a lesson. Select a text. Examine it for the reading strategies you can teach your emergent bilingual children. Consider how you can help them orchestrate the cueing systems (graphophonics, semantics, syntax) in addition to schema (including funds of knowledge). Plan your lesson and videotape yourself teaching it. Watch the video with a colleague. What worked? What could you have done differently? How was students' bilingualism central to the lesson?

3 Review the section on guided reading in this chapter and prepare a lesson. Share the plan with a colleague for feedback and ask her or him to observe you teaching it (do an inter-visitation). Ask your colleague to take notes, focusing closely on your work with emergent bilingual students. After the lesson, ask your colleague what stood out about it and what recommendations she or he has as you continue to develop guided reading lessons for emergent bilinguals. How did students engage in the lesson, using all of their language and social resources?

CHAPTER 5

Translanguaging in Read-Alouds, Independent Reading, and Author and Literature Studies

"There is no such thing as a generic reader or a generic literary work; there are only the potential millions of individual readers or the potential millions of individual literary works. A novel or a poem or a play remains merely ink spots on paper until a reader transforms them into a set of meaningful symbols."

—LOUISE ROSENBLATT

As a teacher of reading, consider carefully how each experience you offer your emergent bilinguals has the potential of supporting them in deepening and expanding their identities as readers. This journey begins with a commitment to knowing children's literature. You set the tone in your classroom by carefully and intentionally planning for translanguaging in each read-aloud. Through these experiences not only do you invite students to enter the world of story, but you also guide them in thinking and talking deeply and critically about books. This path of crafting spaces for emergent bilinguals to strengthen their capacities as readers who can analyze texts critically can continue with author studies, independent reading, and literature studies.

Read-Alouds

Reading aloud is, without doubt, a literacy event filled with complexity and possibility. It offers emergent bilingual children the opportunity to listen to beautifully crafted language, imagine worlds painted by words, study illustrators' interpretations of authors' words, and most importantly, have opportunities to dialogue with others about texts. Read-aloud is a time for the teacher to simply read a book for students' enjoyment. It is a time for us to share a cherished book and the story behind it, or a book that we know the students will just love, or a book that will introduce them to sensitive material. It is a time for students to sit and feel enthralled, invested, and embraced by the story world and carefully crafted language in a book. It is also a time to engage the students in examining a text from a critical stance (Lewison, Leland & Harste, 2008). We might ask the children how certain characters are portrayed. Are there other ways the author could have described this character or captured this place or event? What did you learn about the main character? What did you learn about the other characters?

Reading aloud offers the classroom community the opportunity to develop a shared history of books, as you share stories and texts in a variety of genres with the class throughout the school year (Laminack & Kelly, 2019; Osorio, 2020; Wood Ray, 2001; Smith, 1995). Through read-alouds, children can develop the desire to read independently. After all, to be able to imagine themselves as readers, young emergent bilingual children need to have had experiences with more capable readers inviting them into the world of a story or a nonfiction text. A read-aloud can be the space where emergent bilingual children can fall in love with words and authors, visit new places, understand new ways of being in the world, or find similarities they might have with a character. The read-aloud experience is more powerful if emergent bilingual children are invited to hear stories that offer beautifully crafted language and meaningful experiences, as well as stories that reflect windows into their worlds.

Read-alouds are invaluable, helping to develop readers' identities and interests. Sadly, the space for the read-aloud has dwindled over the years. Although teachers continue to read aloud books in the classroom, the nature of read-aloud has changed in service of other reading priorities. More often teachers are reading aloud books that have been assigned. These books may have been selected because they go with a particular reading strategy or social studies unit. We do not argue that these may not be great books—and may happen to connect to teachers and their students—but that the agency that teachers have in selecting books that are uniquely important to particular students and groups may be dwindling. Often when teaching a particular reading curriculum, teaching points are associated with particular texts, also diminishing the agency that teachers have in selecting or substituting books that may be particularly powerful for a given group of students. Lastly, it is becoming common practice to require teachers to read aloud books for the purpose of teaching reading strategies. We believe that nudging emergent bilingual students into the reading process and bolstering their metacognitive understanding is an incredibly important practice to help students develop into strong readers. Nonetheless, a strategy-based read-aloud has a different purpose than a read-aloud meant to speak directly to the hearts of listeners.

Reading aloud offers the classroom community the opportunity to develop a shared history of books, as you share stories and texts in a variety of genres with the class throughout the school year.

We believe that read-aloud needs to happen every day. In other words, it needs to become a consistent daily classroom ritual. The children need to know it will happen daily—and when it will happen. In a classroom that holds multilingual learners as its members, how the teacher invites them to join the community of readers matters. So while the selection of books is essential, so are the opportunities to understand, study, and respond to the meanings of texts. A teacher who knows his or her students searches carefully for books that offer them both windows as well as mirrors. The read-aloud does not always need to be fiction. The teacher needs to contemplate the purpose of the read-aloud. It might be connected to a thematic study, the class might be doing an author study, or it might fall under a particular genre (e.g., poetry, nonfiction, argumentative writing). It might also be carried out because of an issue the classroom community is experiencing—the loss of a pet, the departure of a classmate who is moving, the need to talk about care and kindness, etc. In this way, the read-aloud functions as a deeply intimate space for emergent bilingual students and teachers to convene around words, topics, illustrations, and ideas (Espinosa & Lehner-Quam, 2019). These are some basic principles of what we hope every classroom aims for in reserving an important space for read-alouds. However, teachers who have emergent bilinguals can also claim space for translanguaging within the read-aloud and stake out this space as a normative one.

A Translanguaging Vision for Read-Alouds

Looking at read-alouds through a translanguaging lens helps us think about read-alouds in several ways. First, it assists us to think about how language is positioned in the book and how it reflects the vision and life of the author and how students can connect to it. Even if the book is entirely in English, it's important to think about how the diverse richness of English is framed in the book and how it reflects the lives of people in the book. For example, Matt de la Peña's (2015) book, *Last Stop on Market Street*, demonstrates alternating varieties of English in authentic and respectful ways. It's important to also think about how the language in the book reflects the languages and cultures of the students in the class. For example, the classic *Abuela*, by Arthur Dorros (1997) seamlessly weaves in phrases in Spanish to convey the experiences of a young girl exploring the city with her grandmother, but so does a more current book by author Meg Medina, *Mango, Abuela, and Me* (2015). Books that capitalize on translanguaging have existed for decades as authors capture how authentic language exists in the world. These books provide wonderful opportunities for students to discuss the reasons why an

Any book and any engagement with a text can provide opportunities for translanguaging.

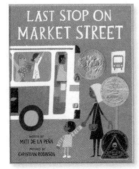

author may translanguage within a book and how the audience experiences this type of text.

Any book and any engagement with a text can provide opportunities for translanguaging, because when we read aloud a book, we are opening up spaces for students to engage in books using their entire linguistic repertoire. Throughout the reading of the book, teachers must think about how they orchestrate opportunities for talk. Multilingual learners need opportunities to leverage their entire linguistic repertoire to make sense of the text and be able to construct new meanings throughout the read-aloud. Students can talk about the topic of the book before they read it, make predictions, and discuss with the teacher some of the things that will happen in the book. Such deep thinking and engagement can happen throughout the read-aloud during Turn and Talk and questioning, in general. Additionally, as students respond to read-alouds, they can also include multimodal approaches, such as dramatizing a scene, engaging in readers' theater, or writing a song inspired by the story.

Before the Read-Aloud

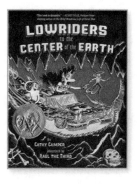

When selecting books for a read-aloud, while keeping in mind the children's needs and who they are, you might select a book where the characters translanguage (for example, *Lowriders to the Center of the Earth* by Cathy Camper and illustrated by Raul The Third). You might invite the children to study the dialogue of the characters in the book. Also, look for authors who use translanguaging to describe objects or places. Study also how authors use translanguaging in their lives. These types of books are particularly important as a way to affirm and expand the children's identities and experiences as readers. They normalize the language practices of bilinguals.

Action 8

Study Your Favorite Books

We all have favorite books and texts that we like to share with our students. These may be texts that you had a connection with for many years or they may be ones that you shared with teachers and peers. However, often we don't pull all of our favorite texts together to see what they represent to our students as a whole. For example, a question such as "How do the read-alouds we choose portray Latinx families and communities?" When I (Laura) asked this question, I knew that I needed to expand the range of books that I hold as my favorites. We also look to Henderson et al.'s (2020) study, in which she examines her classroom library to ascertain its diversity.

For this action, we want you to think expansively about how diversity may appear for emergent bilinguals—considering how the characters in books live out their identities through a variety of factors, including language. For this action, we ask you to gather your favorite texts. Then ask yourself the following questions:

- What do these texts have in common?
- What makes each of these texts different from one another?
- Who are the characters in these texts? (Think about gender, race, socioeconomic factors, sexual orientation, and status, as well as language.)

- What contexts are portrayed in these texts? (urban, rural, school, family structure, etc.)
- What cultures are present, and how are these cultures represented? Do the books reflect my students? Will they enlarge my students' understanding of the world?

Once you identify patterns, think about whether there are gaps. This will help you decide whether you need to look for books with more Chinese characters, or more Latinx girls, or more books with LGBTQ families, or books with families that speak more than one language, etc. Notice the collection of books you have that are written by "own voices." (Corinne Duyvis coined the hashtag movement #ownvoices with the purpose of naming, recommending, and highlighting books about diverse characters that are written by authors who are from the same diverse group.)

Once you know how you can fill the gaps, you can start thinking about where to search for new books that round out your collections. You can start by looking at books that have won awards, asking librarians or colleagues, or following the social media accounts of organizations such as We Need Diverse Books.

Analyzing the Book for Translanguaging Possibilities

As the reader, you will demonstrate for children how to interact with the world of the story. Notice the places where you might stop to invite the children to make a prediction or make an inference. You might want to put a sticky note in these sections to help you remember. Also, note the words in the story that you might need to define for the children before, during, and after reading. Consider carefully the spaces where you will invite the children to share their thinking, always ensuring that their entire linguistic repertoire is part of the meaning-making process. Think about your students and their histories. For example, Laura remembers one year when she had a student, Sara, who arrived from Guatemala at the end of fall. She had never seen or touched snow, so she had no experience with the coldness and the contrasting pillow-like quality of it from afar, compared to the hard whack of a snowball that hits your arm. To understand a book about a frosty winter and the various ways an author might describe snow, Sara needed a multi-layered, firsthand experience with snow.

While the focus of the read-aloud is to invite our students to enter the world of a well-crafted text that has beauty of language, interesting characters, rich descriptions, and a unique plot or structure, we are also demonstrating how fluent, efficient readers read. So, consider demonstrating a think-aloud using the "say something" strategy (see *Reading Revealed*, p. 128), posing a question, making a connection, re-reading a portion, and so forth.

Bilingual teacher Esmeralda Salas showcases an example of a bilingual book that also addresses an important issue.

During the Read-Aloud

As you begin the read-aloud, point out the dedication page by the author and illustrator, if there is one. While often very brief, a dedication offers a glimpse into the author's and illustrator's lives, visions, eras, etc. By helping children notice the dedication, you offer an added opportunity for them to connect with the story they are about to hear. You can then start reading the book with voice and intonation, paying careful attention to the beauty of the carefully crafted language and the plot of the story. Although it is important not to interrupt your read-aloud and disrupt its magic, there should be a few instances in which you stop to share your thinking as a reader or invite your students to share theirs, in particular noticing when the author is weaving her linguistic and social repertoires into the text.

Laura shows a picture of *Molly's Pilgrim* with a caption in Chinese to newly arrived students before the read-aloud, to preview ideas and language.

After the Read-Aloud

Once you finish the read-aloud, carefully consider the questions you pose to the children. Ask open-ended questions so the ensuing discussion provides children with multiple zones of proximal development (Vygotsky, 1978) and thus, with your help, they are able to enter more complex meanings about the story. This part of the read-aloud should be a conversation with students, rather than an assessment of their comprehension of the book.

Discussions after the read-aloud should be thought of as a conversation with students, rather than a time to assess students' comprehension.

The following questions or prompts invite the children to respond. As you introduce each question, you may want to create a chart to keep track of the prompts your students understand and display it in the classroom.

Responding to a Read-Aloud

- What did you notice? I noticed…
  ¿Qué te llamó la atención? Yo noté… Me llamó la atención…

- What do you wonder? I wonder…
  ¿Qué te preguntaste? Yo me pregunto…

- What did you think? I thought…
  ¿Qué pensaste? Yo pensé…

- What part did you like? I liked…
  ¿Qué parte te gustó? Me gustó…

- What did you learn? I learned…
  ¿Qué aprendiste? Yo aprendí…

- What did you discover? I discovered…
  ¿Qué descubriste? Yo descubrí…

- What did you feel? I felt…
  ¿Qué sentiste? Yo sentí…

Responses that promote further dialogue:

- I agree with _____ because _____
  Yo estoy de acuerdo con _____ porque _____

- I disagree with _____ because _____
  Yo estoy en desacuerdo con _____
  porque _____

Portions in English by Karen Smith
(Language Arts course at Arizona State University)

One way to extend the read-aloud across time is to engage children in an author study. An author study is a way to introduce a variety of works by a single author. As a result, students come to know the author as a writer and a person. This is also an opportunity for students to get to know authors who may reflect their identity and help them understand that many types of people can capture their voices in text.

Into the Classroom

Reading Aloud to Emergent Bilinguals

Mr. Peters, an English as a New Language (ENL) teacher, chose *Between Us and Abuela: A Family Story from the Border* (2019) by Mitali Perkins and Sara Palacios for his read-aloud. He shows the second-grade children in his self-contained ENL class the cover page and asks them to describe what they see, using their entire linguistic repertoire. For this purpose, he has asked the children to sit next to a classmate who is bilingual. The children share that there is a child on the floor who is drawing. The other person is sitting on a sofa holding her knitting. Margarita says in Spanish, "Hay un árbol de Navidad." Mr. Peters asks José to translate. He eagerly says, "She said, 'There is a Christmas tree.'" Mr. Peters points to the Christmas tree. Another child adds that there is a lamp, a frame with a picture, a carpet, a cactus, and so on. Mr. Peters asks a child to say all these names in Spanish. Then he asks them if they know where the title is, what it says, as well as where the author's and illustrator's names are. He asks the children to predict what the book might be about, based on the title and their description

of the cover page. The children say that maybe the characters are getting ready for a visit from grandma (la abuela).

Mr. Peters does a picture walk. He invites the children to describe what they notice on each page. He knows that a picture walk is important because it helps the children generate vocabulary collaboratively about the illustrations of the book and positions them as active readers. Next, he reads the story aloud to the children. He has prepared for the read-aloud by reading the book to himself a couple of times. He knows the book well. He has also marked a few pages as places where he will ask the children to make a prediction or an inference about the story. He reads the story with intonation. He adds gestures when appropriate, in order to convey the feeling of the author's words for his audience. He also points to key items in the pictures to facilitate the children's understanding of the story. At one point, he asks, "How do you say *kite* in Spanish?" The children say, "*Cometa, papalote, papelote...*". He reminds them that they will need to create a chart of all the different words that are used in Spanish for *kite*. He stops during the read-aloud to ask the children to share their predictions with a partner, and then he asks two to three partners to share with the whole group. At one point, once they are into the story, he stops and asks them to infer what they think will happen next. Will the main character be able to send the message to Abuela?

At the end of the story, he asks the children open-ended questions:

- What did this story make you think about?
- How did you feel about what happened?
- Did you have a favorite part?
- What surprised you?

He points to the chart, on which these questions are written in English and Spanish.

Once again, he invites the children to share their thinking in their home language. Several bilingual children offer to translate what their peers say.

At the end of the read-aloud, Mr. Peters reminds the children that they can read this book during independent reading time. He also starts a chart with the different words in Spanish for *kite* (e.g., *cometa*, *papalote*, *papelote*, *chiringa*, and *volantín*), and draws a picture of a kite.

Author Studies

Engaged and experienced readers develop relationships with authors. Over time they get to know an author's body of work and style. They also learn about the author's life and about both the struggles and triumphs of being an author. As they read multiple texts by a single author, students can also become familiar with the author's favorite themes. Emergent bilingual children can study authors who offer them reflections of their backgrounds. To get a closer glimpse of how an author study is carried out, let's look at Ms. Sun's class. As we shared earlier, while it is easy to collect works by authors like Eric Carle, Cynthia Rylant, and Dr. Seuss, it is critical that the collection of authors in your classroom library is diverse and representative of the emergent bilingual children in your class (España & Herrera, 2020; Lehner-Quam, West, & Espinosa, 2020).

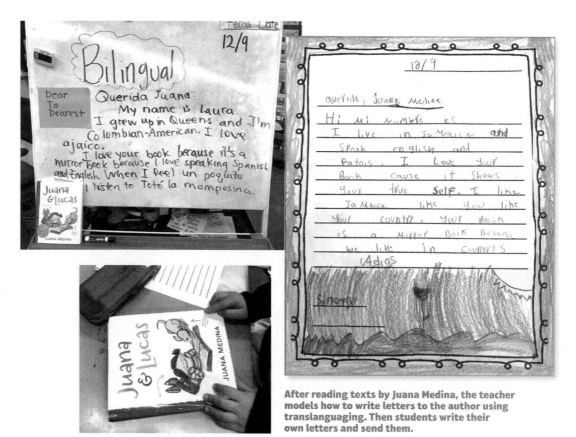

After reading texts by Juana Medina, the teacher models how to write letters to the author using translanguaging. Then students write their own letters and send them.

Into the Classroom
Developing Relationships With Authors

Second-grade bilingual teacher Ms. Sun, believes that in the same way that adults have relationships with particular authors, children also need to begin to form relationships with authors of children's literature. Ms. Sun begins by sharing her own reading life with her students. They know she loves memoirs, poetry, and historical fiction. The children often see some of the books she reads. They know she has some favorite authors. They also know that she eagerly waits for the next books written by her favorite authors. The children also see her reading books in Spanish and English. For this purpose, the teacher selects three or four authors each year whose work the children will get to know in more depth. They have studied the work of Duncan Tonatiuh, Jorge Argueta, Jacqueline Woodson, María Fernanda Heredia, and Pat Mora.

Examples of other authors Ms. Sun wants the children to know about are Hena Khan, Linda Sue Park, Allen Say, Derrick Barnes, Jason Reynolds, Grace Lin, Traci Sorell, and Gene Luen Yang, among others. While Latinx emergent bilinguals are the largest group in the United States, we strongly believe that students need mirrors and windows, and therefore teachers should explore diverse authors' work.

During the last two weeks, Ms. Sun's class has been studying the work of bilingual children's literature author Pat Mora. Ms. Sun selected this author intentionally. In her books, Mora capitalizes on her linguistic repertoire as a writer. Ms. Sun, who has studied

Author studies can happen across grade levels. In this upper grade classroom, they also studied about Pat Mora and engaged capitalizing on their entire linguistic repertoire.

Pat Mora through her websites and articles, shares with her students what she has learned about Mora's life. Her students are familiar with Mora's love for words. They also learn that much of her writing comes from her own experiences, her observations of the world, the places she travels, her memories, the comments she hears, the places she loves, the people in her life, and the cultural traditions she grew up with. Most importantly, they learn that Mora is a reader. Ms. Sun shares with the children that Mora, although she grew up bilingual, never saw herself as a bilingual writer because books that reflected her bilingualism were not available to her at school or even in local libraries.

Ms. Sun introduces the children to Pat Mora's website (patmora.com/books/for-children) and to her collection of books. Among the books written by Mora that Ms. Sun's class reads are: *The Desert Is My Mother/El desierto es mi madre* (2008), *Tomas and the Library Lady* (2000), *The Rainbow Tulip* (2003), *My Singing Nana* (2019), and *Abuelos* (2009). Ms. Sun understands how important it is that children have access to a diversity of voices, in particular voices of authors who in the past might have been silenced. She understands that as their bilingual identities evolve they will often occupy what Mary Louise Pratt (1991) coined as the "contact zone," the borders "where cultures meet, clash, and grapple with each other, often in contexts of highly asymmetrical relations of power..." (p. 34).

Ms. Sun understands that her children will be influenced by the wisdom and ways of being that their various cultures reflect. Their cultural ways of being will also change over time. They learn from Mora that words matter, that we can use them to change our lives and the world. On this day, the children are reading Mora's book *Doña Flor: A Tall Tale About a Giant Woman With a Great Big Heart* (2005). Ms. Sun guides the children in a character study of a powerful Latinx woman who is

bilingual. Together they study the words the author chose to describe Doña Flor. They also discuss how the illustrator portrayed her. Ms. Sun understands that it is by meeting a character like Doña Flor that children grapple with strong characters in difficult situations. In selecting carefully the books she reads to her class, and reading books by a single author who attends to complex themes, Ms. Sun hopes to usher students into a literary world, where they can come to understand the power of literacy to view, critique, and rewrite life situations.

To facilitate discussion and to create a whole-class reference, Ms. Sun creates this chart:

Author Study: Books by __Pat Mora__

Title	Who are the characters? In what languages do they speak?	Does the book have words in other languages? What are they?		Where does the story take place?	What is the story about?	What are questions we have for the author about this book?
A Birthday Basket for Tía	Main character (Cecilia) Mamá Tía They speak Spanish and English	Tía Chica (cat's name) noventa años mamá	bizcochos hierbabuena piñata cumpleaños	Main character's home	When you give a gift to someone you love, you need to think carefully about what you are going to give the person.	Is this a story from your life? Did you grow up speaking Spanish and English?
Doña Flor: A Tall Tale About a Giant Woman With a Great Big Heart	It says Doña Flor spoke every language, including rattler [snake]. In the story she speaks mostly Spanish and English. Other characters: neighbors, her animal friends, the puma	Por favor escuela Mi casa es su casa. pan tortillas ¿Qué pasa? gato	puma coyotes estrellas una amiga luna ¿Dónde estás? amigo mesa	Doña Flor's pueblo (maybe where the author lives)	It is OK to be different. What matters is what is in your heart.	Where did you get your idea for this story? Why did you decide to write that Doña Flor speaks every language?
Tomás and the Library Lady	Tomás Papá Grande Enrique Mamá Papá They speak Spanish and English.	Buenas noches En un tiempo pasado uno, dos, tres, cuatro ¡Qué tigre tan grande! libro Buenas tardes, señora pan dulce		Migrant camp Texas Iowa A library	Everyone can become a reader. The library is for everyone.	Who are other people you would like to write about? Why is the library important to you?

Find a blank form online at scholastic.com/RootedResources.

Over time the children complete the chart and discuss what they notice about Mora's work and her writing style. They discuss how her bilingualism supports her writing.

Ms. Sun also writes down important details the class learns about Mora's life and work. The charts serve the children as points of reference and conversation starters. She also invites the children to explore Mora's work on their own. Then Ms. Sun gathers the Mora books and places them in a basket with her name. Children can revisit these books during independent reading time.

Independent Reading

During independent reading, students embrace their own reading interests and pace their own reading, following guidelines you provide. Students should read books that they can comprehend, that challenge them and offer practice opportunities, and that engage them in topics that matter to them. It is important that the books offer children access to their own linguistic and sociocultural backgrounds. This means that you as a teacher will be providing students with guidelines for selecting books that are just right for them, keeping in mind levels, interest, named language, genres, etc. Usually, teachers conduct whole-group lessons about just-right books so that students construct a common idea of what this means—and then a classroom culture of what it means to be a reader develops.

Children should learn about their teacher as a reader, as we saw with Ms. Sun in the section about author studies. These conversations help the children understand the purposes of why people read. Creating these routines allows students to have time to think about themselves as readers, return the books that they have finished to the library, and pick books that interest them and are just the right fit to read for a given amount of time. When students are fully equipped to read with their book selections and have an adequate number of books to keep them engaged and challenged for a few days or up to a week, it's time for the students to sit and read.

Second-grade teacher Rebecca Quiñones thinks carefully about how her library supports students' independent reading.

Students usually need assistance in planning how they are going to use their reading time. Often teachers remind students of a reading strategy they want the students to practice as they read independently. This strategy strengthens their reading identities—for example, stop to notice the illustrations in the story, or stop and say (jot down) something that I just read and what it made me think about.

At the end of the session, the teacher might take five minutes for a couple of students to share what they focused on as readers. What is critical is that, over time, students figure out that being a reader is valued. Reading independently is more than reading a leveled book. It is about understanding that reading has to be purposeful to the reader and that developing a reader's identity takes time.

How we schedule our independent reading time also matters. For students in kindergarten and first grade, it's best to begin independent reading time with a manageable amount of time, such as five minutes, and gradually increase the amount. As children mature, they will be able to sustain reading for longer

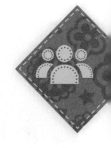

Into the Classroom

Independent Reading in an ENL Classroom

In Xiomara's second-grade ENL classroom, students are beginning independent reading with their own unique selection of books. Students get their book baggie— a plastic bag with five to six soft-cover books—selected for each child based on level, interest, and challenge. Children can either sit at their desks or settle on push chairs and pillows in a carpeted classroom nook. Independent reading time is envisioned as the last phase of the gradual release of responsibility, which means Xiomara has spent time reading aloud to students, engaging them in shared reading and guided reading lessons, as well as discussing the purpose of independent reading. The vision for independent reading is to provide students with the space and time to dig into their reading in ways that are personal and impactful. In Xiomara's classroom, students read to explore characters, topics, and genres of interest and to engage in research. We know that expertise on a topic develops capacity to read more complex texts, as well as to help establish a strong reader's identity.

and longer periods of time. While students are engaged with their reading, you circulate and confer with them, checking in to make sure that the books are appropriate for each student, that they are making expected headway with their books, and that they are understanding and enjoying what they are reading.

While it may seem easy to have students read independently, acquiring enough books that are at the right reading levels, are interesting to children, and that meet their interests is far from easy. Some teachers simplify this challenge by directing students to select only those books that are on the students' reading level. As a result, when students are asked to tell us about themselves as a readers, they often respond, "I am a [level F or H]." Rarely do they mention what they like to read about, what topics they know a lot about, or what genres they are exploring as readers. We urge teachers to stop telling children their level or defining them by their level, but rather to guide students' book choices by their interest *and* their ability to understand the book.

> *Emergent bilingual readers must have a deep connection to what they are reading and also have a bilingual consciousness that guides their reading.*

While leveled books should be reserved solely for guided reading, it is common for many teachers to level the majority of books in their libraries. We do believe that students need to read books that they can understand. If teachers are using leveled books for independent reading, we suggest what Fabienne, a French-English dual-language, bilingual teacher, referred to as "bands of levels." Fabienne advises students to look beyond a single level and, instead, test out books across several levels. Which ones feel like the best fit? It's important to never lose sight of the role of student interest! For all children, but particularly for emergent bilinguals, to fully engage during independent reading time, they must access books about topics that matter to them.

A Translanguaging Vision for Independent Reading

Emergent bilingual readers must have a deep connection to what they are reading and also have a bilingual consciousness that guides their reading. What that means is that students remember that they are readers in both named languages and that they don't shut off their wealth of knowledge *of* and *in* a given language when they are reading. This also means that teachers play an incredibly important supportive role in modeling and encouraging students to understand how to tap into their bilingual powers while they read. This can be done in a number of ways. For starters, teachers can facilitate connections of what they are reading in one language to another. The teacher can also ask students to use their entire linguistic repertoire while they read. For example, if a student runs into a tricky word, the teacher can encourage the student to use more than context clues, but also to search for cognates or similarities to words that are similar to the other language that they speak.

One way students develop strong identities as readers is by engaging in reading together. Reading is a social act, and students can engage with one another around a text through literature studies or, as some refer to them, literature circles.

Literature Studies

A literature study is an intense and in-depth study of one book read by a small group of students—emergent bilinguals and students with different language abilities and backgrounds. It typically lasts three sessions and begins only after the class, together, has experienced many read-alouds and book discussions over multiple weeks—and understands what it means to have a "grand conversation," as educators Peterson and Eeds (2007) argue in their book *Grand Conversations: Literature Groups in Action*. In other words, in the same way children might discuss the plot or a character's transformation in a favorite video, TV show, or movie, they share their understandings about the book, exploring different perspectives, wonderings, and themes. (See page 105.)

A literature study is an intense and in-depth study of one book read by a small group of students.

"Story is an exploration and illumination of life," write Peterson and Eeds (2007, p. 18). Yes! Stories illuminate what it means to be human. Emergent bilinguals need a caring audience who can hear their stories fully. They also need ample opportunities to transact with stories. Some emergent bilinguals come to school having read an abundance of books, while others have heard mostly oral stories. Gallart (1995, 2017) states that classrooms (and schools) should be the spaces that provide access to all children to quality stories, including children's own, as well as opportunities to engage with questions that lead them to deeper interpretations of texts. She argues that classrooms must be places where being a reader matters and where students read for authentic and personal purposes over merely practicing reading skills. It is critical for educators to think about the purposes of reading and how they can best convey and enact these in the classroom. How can you ensure that students, given all their language resources, grow as confident and capable readers and see themselves as readers?

A Translanguaging Vision for Literature Studies

As you help your emergent bilingual children learn the mechanics of reading, you also work hard to help students become readers who enjoy reading, who see the value of it, and who know how to talk about books with others. We argue that emergent bilinguals need access to quality literature in English as well as in the languages they speak at home. In this way, emergent bilingual readers intentionally and strategically use their linguistic repertoire when discussing books. Interpretation is the result of a transactional process in which readers bring meaning to, as well as take meaning from, a text. Children are born "meaning makers" (Wells, 1985; 2009). They need extensive and intensive experiences with quality literature that reflects their linguistic backgrounds.

Children are born "meaning makers."

Through read-alouds, you create a reading environment where you model and invite students to think about authors, texts, and themes. Literature studies complement read-alouds in that they give emergent bilingual children opportunities to attend to deeper layers of meaning in a carefully selected story (Martínez-Roldán, 2005; Smith, 1995). Literature study experiences allow readers to discover that the text has multiple possible interpretations through discussions that bring together students' thoughts and feelings (Peterson & Eeds, 2007).

The three big questions on the next page, developed by Beers and Probst (2017), offer great opportunities for children to think about their responses as readers. We have added the importance of capitalizing on the children's entire linguistic repertoire.

3 Big Questions

What surprised me? ¿Qué me sorprendió?	What did the author think I already knew? ¿Qué es lo que la autora pensó que yo ya sabía?	What challenged, changed, or confirmed what I knew? ¿Qué me retó, me hizo cambiar o confirmó lo que yo sabía?
I was shocked about... Yo estaba conmocionada... **I was surprised when...** Yo estaba sorprendida cuando... **I never thought...** Nunca pensé... **I could not believe...** No pude creer... **Really?** ¿De veras?	**I did not know...** Yo no sabía... **I was confused by...** Yo estaba confundida cuando... **The author assumed...** La autora asumió que... **The author thought...** La autora pensó... **I know...** Yo sé...	**At first I thought... but...** Al principio yo pensé... pero... **I had to rethink...** Tuve que volver a considerar... **The author confirmed...** La autora confirmó... **My understanding changed when...** Mi comprensión cambió cuando... **I was right/wrong about...** Yo estaba en lo correcto/ equivocada cuando...

Before the Literature Study

In a literature study it is important to offer students some choice. In preparing for the literature study, you want to plan intentionally and thoughtfully by reading the book carefully and studying its possibilities. You want to examine the possible interpretations readers can bring. You might analyze the book by asking:

- Who are the characters the readers meet?
- What do they learn about them?
- How do the characters change? What causes the change?
- How are tensions resolved?
- Who is telling the story?
- Where does the story take place? How does the reader know?
- How does time pass in the story?
- How do authors and illustrators show mood?
- What is the symbolism in the story? What is the story really about?
- How can I support the emergent bilingual children's full engagement in this literature study?

During the Literature Study

Participate in each session with genuine interest in what the other members are saying. As needed, support the development of ideas and, if it makes sense, extend them.

At the heart of literature studies is dialogue about the reading. Children can work together to understand complex stories and construct meaning collaboratively. They bring to the text their schema (lived experiences), their sociocultural values and perspectives as well as their linguistic repertoire. The members of the small group unpack meaning through dialogue as they discuss the story. The following is an outline of a way that literature studies might unfold. While the following example is appropriate for students in grades 2–5, it could be adjusted for students who are younger or older.

A Day-by-Day Example
of a Literature Study

Getting Ready

- Mr. Hernandez, a third-grade dual-language bilingual teacher, establishes a group of five students, keeping in mind languages, bilingualism, variety of experiences as book discussants, diverse reading levels, etc.

- He looks for books that offer the readers complexity of plot, authentic characters, the possibility of examining symbolism, etc.

- Mr. Hernandez has selected three or four titles that he has five to six copies of.

Day 1

- Mr. Hernandez offers the children the following choices: *La Mariposa* by Francisco Jiménez (2000), *The Last Stop on Market Street* by Matt de La Peña (2015), *The Other Side* by Jacqueline Woodson (2001), *The Day You Begin* by Jacqueline Woodson (2018), *My Papi Has a Motorcycle/ Mi papi tiene una moto* by Isabel Quintero (2019). (Note: Some of these books are available in Spanish, so he offers them too.)

- The small group of children has time to browse through the books. The group selects one title to read together.

- Mr. Hernandez gives the children the Literature Study Contract (pages 111–112) and discusses it with them.

- The group decides how much of the book they will read before they meet on Day 2. If it is a picture book, the group will read the entire book.

- Mr. Hernandez makes available an audio recording of the book for students for whom the book is too difficult to read independently. If this is not possible, he asks two children (one more proficient than the other) to read the book together. If possible, the teacher can also make the audio recording available in languages other than English that students use.

- The group decides on the homework for session one. The homework is straightforward. Mr. Hernandez asks his students to read the book (or a section of the book) and mark places with sticky notes that they find interesting and want to share with their small group. He also asks them to use a reading notebook to capture their thoughts while they read. Students are encouraged to come prepared to talk about the book. Mr. Hernandez reminds them that they can take notes in their own home language. He reminds them that the goal is to share their thoughts with their peers as they work together to construct meaning and understand the book.

- The children and teacher prepare the Literature Study Contract.

Day 2

- The group meets. Mr. Hernandez talks with the children about expectations for listening and sharing. He also checks whether the children have done their homework and helps those who have not figured out a strategy to make sure they are prepared.

- The children use their notes to talk about the story and to listen to what others have to say. The emergent bilingual children are invited to enter into the dialogue using their linguistic repertoires.

- Mr. Hernandez is both a participant and a note taker. (Mr. Hernandez will need to notice what the participants seem to be drawn to as they talk about the book.) Through careful listening, and because Mr. Hernandez has studied the book carefully, he can add to the discussion in ways to help the children notice more complex aspects about the story.

- At the end of the meeting, Mr. Hernandez briefly reviews the discussion and considers what the group might do for homework for Day 3. A couple of children in the small group will study one or two characters to examine how they evolved throughout the story. Another pair of students examines how the different tensions in the plot got resolved. Another team studies how the author conveys the sense of time and mood in the story. (If it is a picture book, the children can be asked to study the illustrations to determine mood.)

- The children are once again reminded to bring notes, drawing on their linguistic and semiotic repertoires.

Day 3

- Mr. Hernandez helps the children organize their notes from their homework.

- The purpose of this meeting is to guide the children in a discussion that leads them to deeper understandings about the story. They review the expectations for talking and listening to each other.

- The children bring their notes to share, based on the specific homework they were given.

- Mr. Hernandez listens to the children's deeper ideas about what the story is really about, or what the meaning of a particular metaphor might be.

The Next Couple of Days

- Once this group of children finishes their literature study, they might want to celebrate the book using a different medium such as art or theater, and, in response, compose a poem or song, paint a mural, create a diorama, write a brief scene for a play, and so forth.

- The children and Mr. Hernandez reflect on their work during this literature study. He asks them what worked well and what they could do differently next time.

Typically, teachers plan one literature study at a time, while the rest of the class reads independently. Thus, the children might participate in a literature study only three times during the academic year, although it certainly could be more, depending on your choice and the children's interests.

After the Literature Study

After the study, children go back to reading their own books during independent reading time with a stronger reading identity, having experienced the power of literature and the grand conversations that can occur around it (Eeds & Peterson, 2007).

Following is a literature study contract that you can use to help your participating children get organized for a literature study.

Literature Study Contract

Name: _____   Date: _____

I agree to read the book titled/Voy a leer el libro:

_____

I plan to read the book as follows/Planeo leerlo de la siguiente manera:

Day/Día 1	Day/Día 2	Day/Día 3
Date/Fechas: _____	Date/Fechas: _____	Date/Fechas: _____
Example: I will read the book or will listen to it. Ejemplo: Leeré el libro o lo escucharé.	Example: I will reread the book. I will use sticky notes to mark key sections of the pages I want to talk about. Ejemplo: Yo volveré a leer el libro. Usaré notas adhesivas para marcar secciones en el libro sobre las que quiero hablar.	Example: I will read it one more time to make sure I am prepared. Ejemplo: Lo leeré una vez más para asegurarme de que estoy preparado.

I kept closely to my plans/Pude mantener mi plan: Yes/Sí: _____ No: _____

What is something I could do differently? ¿Qué es algo que podría hacer diferente?

_____

_____

_____

Literature Study (Discussion Sessions)

Book/Libro: _____

Name/Nombre: _____ Dates/Fechas: _____

	A	**B**	**C**	**D**	**E**
Brought Book Trajo su libro.					
Was Prepared Vino preparado.					
Participated Participó.					
Completed Assignments/ Terminó las tareas					

Teacher Comments/Comentarios del educador/de la educadora:

_____

_____

_____

_____

Student's Signature/Firma del/de la estudiante

_____

Teacher's Signature/Firma del educador/de la educadora

(Adapted to fit the needs of emergent bilingual students from Karen Smith, Bringing children and literature together in the elementary classroom, Primary Voices, 1995, volume 3, (2), p. 31–32.)

Closing Thoughts

Selecting texts for sharing with your students through read-alouds, author studies, independent reading, and literature studies is at the heart of literacy because these experiences provide students with opportunities to see themselves in texts and enlarge their world. In this chapter, we highlighted and demonstrated how you can engage students both in making meaning and enjoying texts, using their entire linguistic and social repertoires. As they study not only texts, but also why and how authors create texts, students learn how the writing process reflects the inner lives of authors. Also, through literature studies, they come to understand and appreciate reading as a social activity.

Suggestions for Professional Development

A teacher's job is more engaging when the teacher is knowledgeable about children's literature. This knowledge is particularly important for our work with emergent bilinguals.

1 Engage in a study of deeply understanding an author who writes books that feature diversity. This could start by visiting websites that focus on diverse children's literature, such as those that are featured on p. 50. Together with your colleagues, select an author you want to learn more about and that you can share with your children. Visit websites and go to the library to locate the author's books. Set a due date to complete the author's study. Come prepared to share with your colleagues what you learned about the author. Share what you learned about the author's life and what the author says about writing. Select a few books from this author's work that you want to share with your colleagues. Discuss the ways in which this author's work supports your work with emergent bilinguals' reading development.

2 In grade-level teams, brainstorm what makes a good read-aloud book. Bring to this session two or three of your favorite read-alouds for emergent bilinguals. Each grade-level team member shares his or her favorite books and why these books are good choices for emergent bilinguals. Consider the kinds of conversations emergent bilingual children will need to have after a read-aloud in order to get ready for literature studies. Think, in particular, how the activities and discussions that you plan for during

literature studies leverage students' resources. A great place to start is to revisit the different questions about engaging children with literature that we shared in this chapter. The intention of these questions is to facilitate children's entering the world of story (or other types of text), as well as participating critically in discussions.

3 Record a video yourself doing a read-aloud. Examine the video. Pay attention to the ways in which you invite emergent bilinguals to fully participate. What are the strengths you notice? What are areas of improvement?

4 Select with colleagues a book (chapter book or picture book) that will inspire rich literature discussion. Participate in a literature discussion where you challenge yourself to examine the elements of literature. After participating as a reader, consider what kinds of support the children in your class would need in order to participate in literature studies.

5 Ask a colleague to come and observe independent reading time in your class. During a prep time, discuss areas of strength and opportunities for growth, in your colleague's opinion.

CHAPTER 6

Reading Assessment: Seeing the Emergent Bilingual Reader

"I believe we can assess students from a strengths-based perspective, valuing their emerging bilingualism, instead of using a deficit perspective where we only consider what they don't know and can't yet do."

—ELLA, TEACHER OF ENGLISH AS A NEW LANGUAGE

Consider the following two classroom realities:

1. A dual-language bilingual teacher completes running records with her students in English and Spanish. After determining her students' reading levels for both languages, she stores away her notes, not to take out her students' assessments until the next round of running records in the coming months.

2. A teacher is excited to assess a student whom she has seen grow as a reader, both in terms of reading strategies in and enthusiasm toward reading, only to find that he has not "officially" moved to the next reading level. When the teacher looks over the student's miscues, or deviations from the text, she finds that the majority of them had to do with the student's language learning, specifically with verb tenses that are not common in his home language.

Are these scenarios familiar to you? As classroom teachers, we loved teaching reading but found that the assessment of emergent bilinguals was disconnected from our teaching and from what we knew about our emergent bilinguals. We were neither supported nor guided on how to use classroom reading assessments, like running records, to understand our emergent bilinguals' reading. In fact, often the primary focus of teachers when doing reading assessment is determining student reading levels, rather than trying to understand the complexity of how a reader navigates the text.

In this chapter, we first outline foundational concepts about reading assessment for all students before describing how you can incorporate *responsive adaptations*—flexible ways of adapting assessments so that students' multilingual resources are taken into account during the process— so that you can build accurate understandings of emergent bilingual readers.

Classroom Reading Assessment: Purpose and Practices

Assessing students' reading is essential in understanding how to tailor your reading instruction for their continuous development as readers. Classroom-based reading assessments, such as running records, give an abundance of information about students' reading since teachers listen, observe, and document students as they read. At the heart of knowing your students is being an effective kidwatcher (Clay, 2000; Goodman & Owocki, 2002) to gain insights about how your students experience reading. Marie Clay wrote, "There must be times when the teacher stops teaching and becomes an observer, a time when she must drop all of her presuppositions about what this child is like, and when she listens very carefully and records very precisely what the child can in fact do" (1993, p. 3).

When you know your students as readers, you can develop effective, responsive, and appropriate approaches to support them. However, deeply understanding your students is becoming increasingly difficult. Reading assessments are too frequently used to determine students' reading levels and report them to school administrators. Teachers are being told which assessment tools to use, when to use them, how and to whom to report results, and how students should be grouped, based on those results.

The culture around reading assessment, which includes classroom-based reading assessment, often feels more test-based than formative. Teachers are being asked to assess students' reading and then to report scores (as if they were administering a test), rather than to analyze results and use what they learn to enrich teaching. In turn, teachers value and prioritize reading assessments as a tool to obtain students' reading levels rather than as a means to understand the child as a reader.

Assessment Versus Testing

While many people use the words *assessment* and *testing* interchangeably, they are different, with very different effects on instruction. Tests are tools to help us see how our students perform on a range of tasks at the end of a period of study. They are often used to compare the knowledge and skills that students demonstrate against a set of standards. They are most often summative and evaluative—they communicate to teachers, administrators, and parents how well a child performed against what we want them to know and master. On the other hand, formative assessments—such as running records—were created to help us discover what students know how to do and what they may still need to learn. We must advocate for formative reading assessments to be used not for testing but to learn about and know our students.

A Close Look at Running Records

Running records are a type of formative assessment in which a teacher sits down with a child to document his or her oral reading performance, using a standard set of codes. To administer a running record, select a text slightly above a student's instructional reading level. You can choose a text from your classroom library or from a packaged kit. Another option is to use a passage from a long text that the child is currently reading. Ideally, teachers will have a copy or recording sheet of the text the student is reading, so that they can take notes as the child reads. As you listen to the child read the text aloud, take notes on his or her fluency and miscues. (See "Documenting Children's Reading With Running Records" on pages 119–121.) Your notes should also capture the child's interest in and reaction to the text. When the child has finished reading, ask questions to determine what he or she understands about the text. After listening and documenting the students' reading, the work of assessment is not over. In fact, it is just beginning! When you analyze students' miscues based on your understanding of the cueing systems, schema, and context, you can construct a detailed portrait of your students as readers and base your instructional follow-up steps on that knowledge.

Miscue Analysis

All readers make miscues—or deviations from the text—when they read. Miscues are important windows to understand how readers read. Miscues can be categorized into the following three cueing systems: meaning, visual, and syntax. When students read, they need to orchestrate all cueing systems. If a student substituted "cat" for "kitty," the miscue would still make sense. When the miscue the child makes maintains the meaning, it is called a *high-quality miscue*. The student made a miscue, but he or she maintained the meaning of the sentence. For a miscue to be of high-quality, syntax and semantics would go hand in hand, for example kitty and cat are both nouns and have a similar meaning (felines). If the student read "cup" for "cut," the meaning would have changed, and often the syntax has changed, too. This type of miscue is called a *low-quality miscue* because while it has some graphophonic similarity, it changes the meaning. All readers make miscues. At times, a proficient reader might read "this cat" when the text reads "the cat." While this is also a miscue, it does not alter the meaning. "This" and "the" are articles and are not essential to maintaining the meaning in a sentence.

Ken Goodman (1967) developed miscue analysis when he realized that children read words in context and in authentic texts better and more effectively than in isolation. When a teacher analyzes a child's rendition of a text with a miscue ear, the teacher can examine how the child is utilizing each of the cueing systems and make decisions about how to best support the child to become an efficient/effective reader (Wilde, 2000). A miscue analysis stance allows the teacher to determine which reading strategies the child is using well and which the child needs to develop further. Having this understanding of children's strengths and areas of growth allows teachers to identify how they will support students as readers.

Sometimes a child can make a miscue, but in reality, the cause is that the child is bringing his or her entire linguistic repertoire to the reading event, as you will read about in the next section.

Documenting Children's Reading With Running Records

When you listen to students read, how do you document what you hear? Do you listen with a "miscue ear"? A miscue can be a substitution, an omission, an insertion, a reversal, or a nonsense word. In other words, a miscue is any deviation from a text. Making sure that you document these different ways a child reads is important when you look back on your records or when a colleague refers to your notes. However, at the heart of this process is being curious about the nature of the miscues that students make and how these may be either related to reading or to their language development. The following chart is a reference for not only how you can annotate children's reading, but also the questions you can ask to tease out students' instructional needs. Note that we do not emphasize scoring of miscues, but rather the process of learning about students' complex strategies they draw upon as they read. This reference was compiled by pulling together literacy researchers' recent work on how miscue analysis can be adapted for emergent bilinguals (Ascenzi-Moreno, 2018; Briceño & Klein, 2019).

Running Record Annotations & Questions for Analysis for Emergent Bilinguals

Guiding Questions Throughout:
- How can I support this child as a reader (across the linguistic repertoires)?
- How can I support this child's acquisition of language features of a named language?

When the reader…	Use the following annotation	Example	Questions to Ask
Reads each word accurately	Blank or tick mark above each word.	✓ ✓ ✓ ✓ ✓ ✓ ✓ ✓ When I went home, I ate a cookie.	N/A
Substitutes another word	Write the word above the text.	✓ ✓ ✓ ✓ **ate-ed** When I went home, I ate a cookie.	• Does the substituted word make sense? • Is it a verb? Is it an irregular verb that the student doesn't know? • Did the student drop or add an -ed ending? • Does the substitution reflect the features of the child's linguistic repertoire? • Does the child read an initial sound accurately and then substitutes the end of the word with other sounds?
Substitution of a word in another named language	Write the word above the text.	✓ ✓ ✓ ✓ ✓✓ un ✓ When I went home, I ate a cookie.	• Does the substituted word make sense?
Pronounces word differently than the assessor	Write a P above the word.	✓ ✓when ✓ ✓ ✓ ✓ When I went home, I ate a cookie.	• Does the pronunciation affect meaning? • How does the pronunciation reflect the student's knowledge of a given named language?
Self-correct	Write the miscue, then write SC next to the word.	**went SC** **wented** ✓ ✓ ✓ ✓ ✓ ✓ When I went home, I ate a cookie.	N/A
Insertion	Carrot with the inserted word written above it.	**to my** ✓ ✓ ✓ ✓ ✓ ✓ ✓ When I went home, I ate a cookie. ∧	• How does the insertion affect meaning? • How does the insertion reflect the student's understanding of language?
Child appeals for help and you give time for the child to try it out.	Write A	✓ ✓ ✓ ✓ ✓ ✓ ✓ A When I went home, I ate a cookie.	• What strategies do you hear the student using (sounding out, rereading the sentence)? (If they try it out)
Told	Write T above the word for told.	✓ ✓ ✓ ✓ ✓ ✓ ✓ T When I went home, I ate a cookie.	• Does the student know the word that the teacher told them or is it a new vocabulary word for the child?
Omission	Write O or — above the word.	✓ ✓ ✓ — ✓ ✓ ✓ When I went home, I ate a cookie.	• Does the omission affect the meaning of the text? • Does the omission reflect the child's understanding of language (for example not saying a preposition)?
Rereads a word or phrase.	Draw an arrow along the text to represent the repeated phrase.	When I went home, I ate a cookie. ←	N/A

To illustrate how an analysis supports teachers' knowledge about individual students as readers and informs next steps, we present the miscues from two emergent bilinguals, Oscar and Nubia. Oscar was born in the United States and spoke Spanish at home until he started pre-K in a dual-language bilingual program. He is now in second grade. Nubia came from Colombia at the beginning of first grade and is also a second grader. They both read the text *Frogs and Toads Are Cool Creatures*.

From Oscar's differentiated miscue analysis form, we see that his miscues are generally omissions and insertions, although once he also substituted the word *big* for *bulging*. Questions we can ask of Oscar's miscues include: how do the omissions and insertions affect the meaning of the text, and do they reflect his understanding of language? When answering the question, we see that Oscar's omissions do not generally affect meaning and actually may reflect the way that he speaks. If we ask him to reread the word *bulging*, we may find out whether he just looked at the initial sound and then substituted a word, or if it's a new word for him. Based on this analysis, a plan for Oscar is focused primarily on reading objectives: to ensure that he reads all the text on the line efficiently and effectively, to read to the end of the word, and to ask questions such as, "Did what I just read make sense? What would make sense here?"

Nubia's miscues are more reflective of a child who is bringing her entire linguistic repertoire when she reads in her new language. The majority of Nubia's miscues are either substitutions or insertions. When examining the nature

Differentiated Miscue Analysis Form

Name: Oscar	**Grade:**	2
Text: Frogs and Toads are Cool Creatures	**Text Level:**	J

Text/Teacher Documentation of Student Reading:	S/C	M	V	S	L	P
✓ ✓ ✓ ✓ ✓ ✓ ✓ — — Do you want to learn about frogs and toads?						
Let us ✓ ✓ ✓ it Let's jump right in!ᴧ						
Let us ✓ ✓ ✓ ✓ ✓ ✓ ✓ ✓ ✓ Let's start with frogs. Frogs spend some time on land. Frogs						
✓ ✓ ✓ ✓ — ✓ ✓ breathe through their noses. But they also						
✓ — ✓ ✓ ✓ ✓ ✓✓✓ ✓ breathe through their skin when they are in the water.						
✓ ✓ ✓ big ✓ ✓ ✓ Frogs have big, bulging eyes. Their special						
✓ ✓ them ✓ ✓ ✓ ✓ ✓ eyes help frogs see well when they are in						
✓ ✓ the water.						
✓ ✓ — — ✓ ✓ ✓ ✓ Frogs shoot out their long, sticky tongues to						
lots of ✓ ✓ ✓ ✓ ✓ ✓ ✓ grabᴧfood. ZAP! They eat insects, spiders, and						
— ✓ little fish.						

Types of Miscues
S/C = Self Correction
M = Meaning
V = Visual
S = Syntactical
L = Language
P = Pronunciation

of the substitutions, we can ask, does the substitution make sense, and how does it reflect her language development? We can see that the first substitution is the word *y* in Spanish that is a translation of the word *and* in English, thus preserving the exact meaning of the sentence. Also, we see that some of the substitutions may be reflective of a different way of saying the words from the assessor, such as *shut* for *shoot*, and *steeky* for *sticky*. Lastly, Nubia says "spent-ed" for "spend," in which she added an *-ed* to the end of the verb. She also inserts "in the" instead of the preposition *on*. This analysis reveals that Nubia is capitalizing on her entire linguistic repertoire as a reader.

Next steps for Nubia include learning to fine-tune her understanding of how sounds compare between her two named languages. She can learn to internalize the question, "How do the letters sound differently in each language, and how can I use that when I read?" She also needs support in learning how to use prepositions in English, in different circumstances.

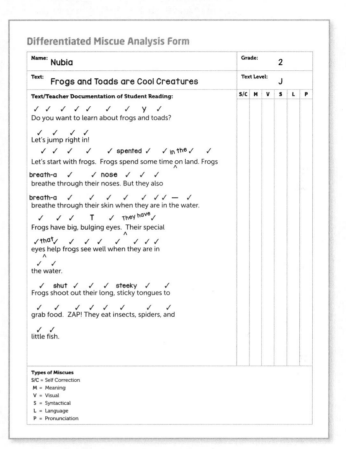

We hope you can see through these examples that the purpose of a running record with a miscue ear is to deeply examine the child's reading of a text and, in this case, how this process is unique for emergent bilinguals who often read in a new language. We urge teachers not to see the purpose of a running record as solely to determine a level. In fact, teachers can use this information and have a reflective conversation with the child about the child's use of reading strategies (Goodman, Martens, & Flurkey, 2016).

Assessments and Translanguaging

While reading assessments provide us with a wealth of information about our students, teachers who work with emergent bilinguals must know how to use these assessments to understand both students' reading *and* language development (Ascenzi-Moreno & Quiñones, 2020; Ascenzi-Moreno, 2016; Briceño & Klein, 2019). Running records can offer teachers a way to understand how emergent bilinguals read, if the process takes account of their bilingualism (Ascenzi-Moreno, 2018). If we want to learn about how emergent bilinguals read, then we should make sure we adapt reading assessments to ensure that bilingual readers can demonstrate what they know, using all of their language resources (Bauer, Colomer, & Wiemelt, 2018; Mahoney, 2017). In this section, we outline the reasons why reading assessments, as they currently are implemented in classrooms, do not accurately capture what students know, and introduce how responsive adaptations or shifts that are attuned to emergent bilinguals' multilingual profiles can be used to build a more accurate profile of bilingual readers.

> *While reading assessments provide us with a wealth of information about our students, teachers who work with emergent bilinguals must know how to use these assessments to understand both students' reading and language development.*

The Need for Adapting Reading Assessments for Emergent Bilinguals

Generally, reading assessments do not take into account emergent bilinguals' simultaneous development of language and reading. This has been well documented; in fact, researchers Ken and Yetta Goodman (1991, 2014) identified issues of miscues due to the linguistic background of the reader many years ago. While emergent bilinguals rely on the three cueing systems previously described (syntactic, semantic, and graphophonic) and schema when they read (Goodman, 1996) as integral to their construction of meaning as readers, these cueing systems may not account for language-related errors nor students' multilingual meaning making of text. When reading in a new language, emergent bilinguals apply their knowledge of these cueing systems differently than monolingual students. For example, students who are just gaining knowledge of the way English is structured will have a harder time using syntactic (or knowledge of how language works) cues to read in

English (Avalos, Plasencia, Chavez, & Rascón, 2007). Similarly, students who are unfamiliar with phonics will have a harder time using graphophonic awareness to support their reading of challenging words. Lastly, emergent bilinguals who are acquiring vocabulary will have problems putting into play their semantic cueing system, as they are still acquiring nuanced word knowledge that will help them read proficiently (Briceño & Klein, 2019).

Emergent bilinguals may make miscues that are a result of being language learners and thus simply making meaning of text multilingually. For example, students acquiring a new language may make mistakes with verb tenses when reading in a new language. It is important for teachers to be attuned to how students' home language may impact their new language production. Teachers can spot trends in student reading in order to determine whether the issue is reading-based or can be supported through language development.

It's important to know how knowledge of students' home language may influence reading in the new language. It matters that the teacher's stance towards these miscues is one of curiosity and that these miscues are seen as a result of students' knowledge base, rather than his or her lack of knowledge. The perspective must be one of strength (Himley & Carini, 2000; Minor, 2019). Goodman (1996) strongly argued that readers want to make sense and bring their capacities as language users to this construction of meaning. It is important that the teacher thinks about why the child made this miscue. What was the child trying to do? For ENL teachers and general classroom teachers, this means they must become familiar with the structure of the languages that their students speak. For teachers in dual-language bilingual classrooms, teachers should understand the structure of the two languages that they teach. In the chart below, see examples of the effect that Spanish may have on English reading. However, we want to emphasize emergent bilinguals acquire reading across languages, and that reading in one language should not be thought of as in service of reading in another language. Rather, reading can be developed across languages.

Examples of Spanish-Language Structures
That May Affect Reading in English

Spanish-Language Structure	How It May Affect English Reading or Speaking	Example
Pronouns are optional with verbs: Quiero comer (I want to eat).	Students may omit a pronoun.	**Text reads:** I love lollipops. **Child says:** Love lollipops.
Idioms: Tengo 10 años. (Literal translation: I have 10 years. Meaning: I am 10 years old.)	Students will use language structure when reading.	**Text reads:** She is 10 years old. **Child says:** She has 10 years old.

In addition, reading assessments are often equated with proficiency in a given language. This is reflected most clearly in the last step of a reading assessment—the comprehension questions that students answer to demonstrate understanding of a text. Very often children who read a book in a given language are asked to solely respond to the book in the same language of the book. This means that these students may not be able to express the fullness of what they know, when limited to expressing themselves in one language. Teachers then may conclude that the students do not understand the text.

Multilingual, Strength-Based Responsive Adaptations

When assessments are viewed through the lens of translanguaging, we can find out about the full span of students' reading knowledge and skills when they bring all of their resources to an assessment. In what follows, we highlight *responsive adaptations* for each component of a running record assessment. Responsive adaptations are flexible ways of adapting assessments so that students' multilingual resources are taken into account during the process (Ascenzi-Moreno, 2018). These adaptations were developed by watching teachers who work extensively with emergent bilinguals. We showcase the work of three teachers: Ella, an English as a New Language (ENL) teacher who works with students, providing in-class and out-of-class support, and two elementary dual-language, bilingual teachers, Anaïs and Fabienne, who teach in a French-English, dual-language bilingual program.

The cultural relevance of books used during reading assessments deeply affects student comprehension and reading accuracy.

Responsive Adaptations for Introducing Texts

Teachers who regularly assess the reading development of emergent bilinguals know that lack of background knowledge and unfamiliar vocabulary in texts pose challenges for emergent bilinguals. As Ebe (2010) and Kabuto (2017) note, the cultural relevance of books used during reading assessments deeply affects student comprehension and reading accuracy. The following responsive adaptations can be used at the start of an assessment when introducing the text. They can be given by the teacher either in English, or using any feature from their linguistic repertoire.

- Reintroduce vocabulary in the text.
- Point out culturally specific terms.
- Provide background knowledge specific to the text.

Into the Classroom

Building Background Knowledge and Vocabulary

Second Grade

Anaïs, a second-grade teacher in a French dual-language program, introduced the book *Mud Tortillas* (Flores, 2004) to one of her French-speaking second graders. This book is about two Mexican American sisters who decide to make tortillas out of mud. Rather than following verbatim the introductory text that was provided to the teacher from a running record kit she was using, Anaïs

decides that her introduction will differ based on her students' backgrounds. Because she knew that one student would not be familiar with tortillas, she made an explicit connection by relating to the student that tortillas are like "salty crêpes." This was done in French to facilitate a quick connection for the student. Although she didn't do this, the teacher could have also shown her a picture of both crêpes and tortillas, so that the student could also understand the similarity through a visual connection.

Fifth Grade

Ella, an English as a New Language (ENL) teacher, provided Yadira, a recently arrived fifth grader from Central America, with background about the text and reintroduced vocabulary before informally assessing her reading. While Ella doesn't use a running record, she uses a guided reading text to listen to her students read with a "miscue ear," because Ella knows it is important to continually assess students authentically. The text that Yadira was to read presented a story about two cousins, one from Vietnam and the other from the United States. To support Yadira's background knowledge, Ella first showed a map indicating where Vietnam is located. Ella then quickly reviewed some words that she had preselected; these words were chosen because Yadira had practiced them before, but they were still relatively new to her.

The tweaks in the introduction that both Anaïs and Ella made provided students with culturally relevant background knowledge including vocabulary, concepts, and terms that assist emergent bilinguals in comprehension. These types of adaptations are simple, yet acknowledge and anticipate that students come to reading instruction with different (not deficient) resources. When we conduct reading assessments, we want to make sure that differences do not impact our view of students' overall reading abilities.

Building Background Knowledge and Vocabulary Knowledge Before the Assessment

In addition to pointing out words that the teacher knew the student needed to review, Ella also pointed out terms that she anticipated would be unfamiliar to Yadira because of their cultural specificity. For example, she highlighted for Yadira that the character in the story was named "Ha." Ella said to her student, "I want to show you a name. It's the name *Ha*. It's kind of a different name." Ella's teaching decision to point out this unfamiliar name and provide some background is important since teachers who work with emergent bilinguals may often focus on culturally specific errors, such as

names, when students read rather than anticipate them (Brown, 2013).

We now move onto how teachers responsively adapted the next phase of reading assessments—the documentation of student reading. All of these responsive adaptations can happen using students' linguistic repertoire. Consider the following examples: An emergent bilingual reads a text in Spanish and answers comprehension questions in English, or an emergent bilingual child reads in English and makes miscues that reflect his relatively new knowledge of English and solid knowledge of Spanish.

An English as a New Language teacher previews concepts and vocabulary for a student before an informal reading assessment.

Responsive Adaptations for Listening to and Documenting Student Reading

In this section, we describe two responsive adaptations for listening to and documenting oral reading, which can occur regardless of the language in which a child reads. That said, they're easier if you know the child's language.

- Document if and when the student's miscues are related to language.
- Provide the student with vocabulary support in his or her home language during reading.

When teachers listen to students read, they also take notes and document how students are reading. Teachers will note the miscues that students make, or self-correct when they read. Teachers also pay attention to how the students read fluently and the reactions that they have as they read. When students are learning two or more languages, their miscues reflect the knowledge across two languages (Briceño & Klein, 2019; Escamilla et al., 2014; Goodman, 1996). To address this issue, Fabienne, who teaches students in English and in French and is familiar with the types of typical errors that students makes, stated that when she listens to students who are learning to read in French, she listens to how the student sounds out words, and takes notes on potential teaching points to support their acquisition of French, rather than counting students' ways of sounding out words as errors (interview, 12/01/2016).

Ella, an ENL teacher, took this approach further. She started to use a reconfigured documentation sheet, which takes into account miscues that are specific to students who are learning to read in a given named language. This documentation sheet, the Differentiated Miscue Analysis Form (used with permission *Language Arts* Journal, Ascenzi-Moreno, 2018) has a column for "pronunciation," or the way that emergent bilinguals sound out words, and another one for "language." When using this documentation sheet, Ella was able to collect detailed information about student reading and differentiate miscues that were related to language acquisition from those that were reading-related. Briceño & Klein (2019) further define the types of language-related miscues that students most often make, including with verb tenses, prepositions, and plurals.

In the following example, Ella listens to Santiago read from the Developmental Reading Assessment (DRA). As reported elsewhere (Ascenzi-Moreno, 2018), Ella carefully listens to and dutifully records Santiago as he reads (see form at right). Then, after he finishes reading, she goes back to ask him for clarification. Ella has marked Santiago's miscues as language-based because she knows that his understanding of what he reads matches the text, although the sounds do not yet match conventional English.

Another practice common among teachers is to provide students with vocabulary support during student reading. During reading, emergent bilinguals may appeal for a definition of an unknown word. For example, during one observation of an English-dominant fifth grader in a French dual-language bilingual classroom, Robert could read the French word *rie* (subjunctive in French: he may laugh) but didn't understand what the word meant. Fabienne responded by acting out the definition.

Differentiated Miscue Analysis Form

				Grade:		
Name: Santiago				5		
Text: A Giant in the Forest				Text Level:		

Text/Teacher Documentation of Student Reading:	S/C	M	V	S	L	P
PAGE 4						
Every week the little boy's mother gave [S/C]	I					
him a big bar of soap. Then she sent [bear]						I
him to the lake to take a bath.						
"You'll be safe in the lake because the [You]				I	I	
giant can't swim," she always said. "But						
don't forget to be home before dark."						
PAGE 5						
One day when the little boy was going to						
take his bath, he saw a baby bird on the [beard]						I
ground. It had fallen out of its nest. [fallen]						I
The boy put the bird back in its nest. [the]				I		

Types of Miscues
S/C = Self Correction
M = Meaning
V = Visual
S = Syntactical
L = Language
P = Pronunciation

You can download a blank **Differentiated Miscue Analysis Form** at scholastic.com/RootedResources. (Copyright 2018 by the National Council of Teachers of English. Used with permission.)

Conventionally, when students appeal for assistance, teachers document this with an "A" for an appeal and a "T" for a word that was told. Both of these behaviors count as errors. However, it is clear from the example provided that Robert could decode the word but needed help understanding the meaning of the word. Rather than signifying a reading error, this type of appeal signals a language-based need.

While listening to student reading, teachers kept in mind that emergent bilinguals are language learners, regardless of the language they are learning, and that their knowledge of the intricacies of sounds, word meanings, and expressions is growing day by day. Just like all readers, their miscues are reflective of their knowledge of language. This knowledge—that students are growing as language learners— affected both how teachers documented student reading and how they responded to their students' appeals for language-based help.

Once teachers are aware of how acquiring the features of a named language affects reading, they can use the documentation of student reading to engage in an analysis that distinguishes which miscues are the result of language development, and which are the result of developing reading abilities.

Responsive Adaptations for Retelling and Answering Comprehension Questions

Teachers of emergent bilinguals want to know whether students understand the text, even if they cannot relate their comprehension entirely in one language. Therefore, they employed the following responsive adaptations:

- Invite/allow students to use their entire linguistic repertoire.
- Reformulate questions to make them comprehensible to students.

Fabienne, a fifth-grade French/English dual-language, bilingual teacher, explains her view on students' responses in their home language to comprehension questions:

> "I note that although they responded in English, it shows that they understood the question. It's fine for me. It means that they are lacking in vocabulary, but they have that comprehension. The problem is in retelling; they don't have the language to do that. We must be flexible, case by case."

Fabienne emphasizes that many of the students use a multilingual repertoire to respond to comprehension questions. This reflects that they experience meaning making as a reader by drawing upon their entire linguistic repertoire.

Fabienne also notes that she sometimes adapts the comprehension questions that may be included in a recording form. She notes that sometimes comprehension questions may be worded in a way that is confusing to emergent bilinguals. Teachers can think about the purpose of the question. Is the purpose to ask students for their literal understanding (for example, to find out the name of a character or to find out whether they know the plot of the story), to make inferences, or to make connections? Is it to assess the retelling of the plot of the story? Then the teacher can ask what vocabulary or context or genre may be difficult for the student to understand and consider how to rephrase it so it is easily understood by the students.

Fabienne speaks to the importance of ensuring that the comprehension questions we ask during an assessment are comprehensible and that students have opportunities to answer them, using all of their language resources.

Responsive Adaptations for Providing Students With Feedback

Providing supportive feedback to emergent bilinguals to help them understand their own reading process is a critical last step. We offer two suggestions:

- Be clear about the reading or language behaviors and goals students should focus on to improve their reading or language abilities.
- Teach self-evaluation skills that assist them in making good choices when they select books independently.

Reading conferences are known to help teachers track and scaffold student reading by providing targeted feedback to students (Taberski, 2000 and 2010; Stephens, Harste, & Clyde, 2019; Scharer, 2016) so they can become effective and efficient readers. Upon completing reading assessments, teachers usually provide students with brief feedback. Teachers can provide concise, targeted feedback that clearly communicates to emergent bilingual students their strengths and areas to work on, either as a reader or in language development. This intentional way of providing feedback, with an eye for reading and for language, requires that teachers view students' performance during a running record with multiple, but complementary lenses that builds upon children's strengths.

For instance, Ella says to one of her younger students, "One of the things that I noticed that was tricky for you were the words like *kicked* and *tossed*—words that ended with *-ed*. We can talk about what sounds to make when we read those." This brief feedback focused on language demonstrates that teachers can provide support to emergent bilingual students on their language growth, which will ultimately impact their reading. Teachers could also start their feedback to students by highlighting what they are able to do in reading and extend this to other skills that are developing. For example, "I noticed how you did a great job of relating the story to your own life. When you are reading this next book, I want you to think about how you can make connections to other aspects of your life and the world, regardless of what language these things happen in."

Typically, teachers provide students with feedback about their reading level and how this impacts their independent book selection. We ourselves have engaged in and viewed many teachers telling students, after the completion of a reading assessment, something along the lines of, "You are now at Level G. Now you can pick three books from the G bin in the library." The teachers featured in this chapter were aware that even though their emergent bilinguals may have "reached" a given reading level as a result of this reading assessment, this did not mean that they should stick to books at that level for their independent reading.

For the purposes of accountability, teachers would note students' independent reading levels, but the teacher would intentionally work with the student to select a book or books from a variety of topics, genres, and levels that would match the student's reading level, interest, and genre. For example, Fabienne says that she offers students "bands of levels" that include interests, which provide students with guidance to read above and below their independent reading level as determined by the reading assessment, as well as opportunities to explore topics they are interested in. Fabienne does this so that her fifth-grade students can develop agency and critical thinking about selecting and reading different types of texts, including a variety of topics, genres, interest, and language difficulty. In other words, the teacher needs to carefully consider all the dimensions at play when selecting texts so that students become aware of what it means to make appropriate choices as readers.

The goal of these responsive adaptations for emergent bilinguals is to be seen and known by teachers as readers when they bring their entire linguistic and social repertoire to reading. We intentionally do not include a section on determining reading level from assessments because we want to emphasize that teachers must bring their knowledge of emergent bilinguals and reading to the assessment process to learn about the emergent bilingual child as a reader, rather than following procedures to determine their level. However, if you do determine a reading level or use a system of leveling books designed by someone else, we recommend that you take a translanguaging stance along with your knowledge of the reading process, and thus do not penalize students for language-based miscues. The following chart summarizes the responsive adaptations introduced in this chapter.

A Multilingual, Strength-Based Framework for Formative Reading Assessments

Step	Responsive Adaptation	What Is the Purpose of This Adaptation?
Introduce the Assessment	Introduce story structure to students. Make culturally relevant connections/position difference. Introduce and revisit vocabulary.	To clarify themes or topics in the story which may be unfamiliar to students To ensure that students are reminded of new vocabulary prior to reading
Listen to and Document Student Reading	Create and use a column for language features.	To provide teachers with a way to determine whether miscues are reading- or language-related
Have Students Retell and Answer Comprehension Questions	Rephrase questions. Invite students to retell or answer questions, using any features from their language and social resources.	To provide students with alternative wordings of comprehension questions that target their level of understanding To provide students with opportunities to use their entire linguistic repertoire as they read
Determine Reading Level	Calculate reading level, taking into account language learning (excluding language-based miscues).	To determine whether miscues are language-related and therefore should not be counted toward total number of miscues
Give Feedback to Students	Focus on both language and reading teaching points.	To provide guidance to students that target both their language learning and reading

Action 9

Take Running Records With Responsive Adaptations in Mind

Now that you know what running records are and understand their potential as well as the challenges they present for assessing emergent bilinguals, we invite you to try out some responsive adaptations. Select an emergent bilingual student about whose reading you are concerned. It would be great if you selected a student with whom you did the Burke Interview (discussed in Chapter 4). Ask the emergent bilingual student to find books in the class that he or she finds easy, just right, and challenging. Talk with the student about this selection of books. Ask the student if there is a favorite topic that he or she likes to read about (e.g., volcanoes, sharks, baseball). Ask the student to read the "just right" book to you. Listen with a "miscue ear" (attending to which cueing systems the student uses and doesn't use). At the end of the reading, talk about the content of the text with the student. As a teacher, reflect upon these questions:

- What do I notice initially about this reader?

- What do I notice about the books the child selected?

- How does the child navigate the "just right" book?

Next, prepare a text that you think is a bit above the student's "just right" book. Make sure it is culturally and linguistically appropriate. Make a copy or type the text to use for the running record. Review the marks used when you document the students' reading, such as omit, reread, pause, partial word, and multiple attempts, among others. Remember that you can also document students' language-related errors and how they express their understanding, using their multilingual repertoire with the Differentiated Miscue Analysis Form. When you are not sure of the type of error a student made, you can ask him or her for clarification. For example, you can ask a child what a word means or ask a child to reread parts of a text.

You should also prepare some comprehension questions. Ask the student to tell you what the story was about. What happened in the story? Invite the student to use his or her entire linguistic repertoire when responding. We recommend you prepare an outline of the story. This way you can check the student's comprehension with more ease.

Once the student is done, look at the patterns of the student's miscues, and think about how the student may have made language-related errors. This is an opportunity to learn about the student as a reader. For example, you may want to ask yourself the following questions:

- Which cueing system is the student overusing or underusing?

- Is the student overusing the graphophonic cueing system at the expense of meaning and knowledge of language?

- What reading strategies does this emergent bilingual student need to develop further?

- What conversations can I have with this student, a small group, or the whole class about what reading is?

- What reading strategies mini-lessons can I create as a result of this informal reading assessment?

- In what reading group would it make sense to place this particular emergent bilingual student?

- What texts should I make available to this student?

- What steps can I take to ensure that the emergent bilingual students feel comfortable capitalizing on their entire linguistic repertoire when reading?

- What feedback can I provide to students that assists them with both reading and language development?

- Were there any ways that I wished I could have learned about the student, but didn't?

- Based on my implementation of this assessment, what new responsive adaptations might I try so that students can enter into the reading along with all of their language practices?

Closing Thoughts

For emergent bilinguals, a complete and accurate portrait of student reading (Afflerbach, 2016) can be revealed when teachers invite students to draw upon all of their language and social resources as they read. Formative reading assessments, which acknowledge that students are multilingual and that their multilingualism affects their reading, allow teachers to develop knowledge about students as readers and identify multiple ways to support their reading and language growth. Teachers can best support their emergent bilinguals as readers when they understand, implement, and remain committed to assessment practices that make room for and value the multilingual practices of their students.

Suggestions for Professional Development

1 Think about what you could do when introducing a text to students to read. What will assist the student to read and comprehend the book? Remember that Ella and Anaïs introduced both words and concepts prior to reading the book. What words would you introduce? Would you introduce visuals? Which ones, and why? Which concepts would you explain, and how would you explain them? How do you encourage students to use their entire linguistic repertoires during the introduction?

2 Select a text with a colleague. It can be a book that you have in a class or a text from a formative assessment kit. If you are using a book, you can create your own comprehension questions. If you are using a running record from a given kit, it will come with questions to ask the student at the end of the reading. Analyze these questions with the emergent bilingual student in mind. For example, would the phrasing be clear to the emergent bilinguals? If you are bilingual, would you rephrase the questions in the language other than English? How do you communicate with students that you would welcome them to respond with their entire linguistic repertoires? If you do not speak the language of the student, how could you support her translanguaging during her retell? For example, could you audio-record the student? Or ask her to write her answers and have someone help you to read them? Think about and plan one or two new ways that you will ask students to respond to the text, using all of their language features.

3 Bring your results of the adapted miscue analysis or running record of the child to discuss with a colleague. Use the Differentiated Miscue Analysis Form presented in this chapter. While you are analyzing your notes, pay attention to the ways that students' language features appear in their reading. What do you think these features mean about their reading or their language learning? What do you learn about this reader? What would be your next instructional steps to support this particular emergent bilingual reader? (Think not only about discrete skills but about the reader as a whole.) If you asked the child the questions from the Burke Interview, which connections could you make about the child as a reader between these findings and your analysis of the child's adapted miscue analysis or running record?

PART III

Writing Into Understanding

▶ **VIDEO LINK**
You will find links to videos with the authors at scholastic.com/ RootedResources.

CHAPTER 7

The Writing Process for Emergent Bilinguals

"What if students did not have to encounter writing instruction informed only by monolingual values and language designations such as ESL? What if, instead, through the integration of families', teachers', and students' linguistic histories and the sharing of linguistically diverse experiences and literature, students composed in contexts where translingual approaches were alive—that is, normalized, studied, discussed, valued, and appropriated for all students' writing?"

—ANGIE ZAPATA and TASHA TROPP LAMAN

As writing teachers, we start by supporting *the writer*—we focus on the child's strengths and areas of need. We invite emergent bilingual children to discover the power of writing, to believe they have something important to say that an audience will want to hear, and to craft their writing so that they convey their message in powerful ways. Sadly, in spite of all we know about how children become writers, in many classrooms writing is too often taught using prepackaged, standards-based genre studies, which may or may not connect to students' lives. We believe that children must learn to write in a variety of genres and that their writing should be developmentally, culturally, and linguistically appropriate. We also believe that instruction should focus on developing a strong writing identity and an understanding that one's writing is more powerful if it has a purpose and conveys the author's authentic meaning to the intended audience. If we recognize children as writers and thinkers right from the start, they figure out that they do have something important to say and work very hard to say it clearly. In the case of emergent bilingual students, we argue for the importance of teachers taking a translanguaging stance and pedagogy during all aspects of writing instruction.

Invite emergent bilingual children to discover the power of writing, to believe they have something important to say that an audience will want to hear.

Because writing instruction is often so squarely focused on genre (e.g., how-to books, small moments/personal narrative, descriptive reports on an animal, and so on), many teachers carry out instruction in the most efficient way possible, without considering what it means to support the emergent bilingual child as a writer. In extreme cases, they select a topic (e.g., how to make a sandwich), and the entire class writes about it, rather than taking the time to allow students to choose a topic they would like to write about. In essence, they teach the steps, rather than focus on the writer's meanings and intentions. Calkins (1983), Graves (1983), and Wood Ray and Cleaveland (2018) remind us that it's important to teach the *writer*, not the writing, and focus on supporting a child's writing identity, as well as finding ways for his or her voice to become stronger. Minor (2019), while not referring to writing, per se, urges us to make our teaching truly meaningful and motivating to children, and relevant to their lives. We want for each student to both develop his or her skills and abilities and feel invested in becoming an engaged and thoughtful writer.

How Do Emergent Bilinguals Experience Writing?

At its core, writing is the creation of meaning (Berthoff, 1981; Hudelson, 1989, 2000, 2005). Writers learn how writing works and what it is within their cultural contexts at home, at school and in the classroom, and in their communities and the larger world. While at home, emergent bilingual children may learn that writing has a purpose and an audience and that their bilingualism is part of their lived experience (D'warte, 2014); but at school, they often learn that their only audience is the teacher, who, for the most part, expects them to write in

English. Students view the teacher's job as primarily to correct and grade their work, but rarely to respond to it in a dialogical, or responsive, manner. School offers limited opportunities for emergent bilingual students to seek the support and guidance of an authentic audience (teachers, peers, and others outside of the classroom), as students attempt to clearly convey their ideas. They seldom learn that writing can be a process of discovering what one means (Hudelson, 2000). Anne Haas Dyson (2015) states that under these circumstances, instead of learning to write, children learn to negotiate "how to do school" because, sadly, writing at school is often only about writing the correct answers or simply following the teacher's directions.

Teachers' beliefs about the teaching of writing have profound implications for how children understand writing (Hudelson, 2005). To truly know how the emergent bilinguals in our classes experience writing, we can ask ourselves the following:

- What are the purposes for writing I offer in my class?
- Do my students have opportunities to write for authentic audiences?
- In what ways do I support the development of the emergent bilingual writer's ideas?
- In what ways do I invite emergent bilingual students to bring their entire linguistic repertoire so that they can fully construct meaning as writers and thinkers?
- In what ways can translanguaging in writing offer emergent bilingual students at all levels opportunities to express themselves and what they know?

Children need opportunities to write for particular purposes and audiences by capitalizing on their entire linguistic repertoires (D'warte, 2014; Velasco & García, 2014). It is only then that they will be able to write for self-expression, to document and present their learning in a content area, to compose in different genres capturing the linguistic practices of their communities, to respond and examine literature, to advocate for issues that matter to them in order to create a more just world, and to craft their writing in ways that engages them in living a literate life (Edelsky, 2003). While it is evident that emergent bilingual children can benefit from explicit instruction and scaffolding, they also need to learn that conversation, collaborating, receiving feedback, discussing writing with others, and examining the work of published authors are important recursive components of the writing process (Espinosa, 2006; Espinosa & Hudelson, 2007).

Emergent bilingual children need to know that their voices matter and that their voices can be developed—that writing can help them make sense of the world as they use it to learn and wonder about them. Clearly, the only way to accomplish that is to invite them to consider new ways of using language as they bring their entire selves into their experiences as writers (Horner, Lu, Jones, & Trimbur, 2011).

Writing as a Unified, Complex Process

A revolution, spearheaded by Donald Graves, began in the 1970s. Graves viewed children as natural writers and urged teachers to re-envision their writing instruction and classroom environment to support their students' growth as writers. Prior to that, writing was taught primarily using a series of prompts and exercises that meant little to children. It was thought that writers develop incrementally from writing letters to words to sentences to paragraphs, and finally, to complete pieces. Young children who struggled to spell were forced to write words and practice skills until they could "really write." Graves's work pushed against those practices and promoted the view that all students, from kindergarten to high school, could engage in writing when they learned the writing process—when they thought about what was personally meaningful to them, when they paid attention to the craft of writing as they read well-written texts, and when they spent time writing, talking about their writing, and sharing it. At the heart of this work is the belief that every student has something meaningful to say in writing and that the writing process is critical to their growth.

Since then, many writing scholars and educators have explored how we can deepen our understanding of the writing process and support students in all grades to write authentically in multiple genres (Fletcher, 2001, 2017; Heard, 1999, 2016; Wood Ray, 1999, 2010). Researchers have also focused on the writing process and emergent bilinguals (Edelsky, 2003; Edelsky & Jilbert, 1985; Fu, 2009; Hudelson, 1989, 2000, 2005; Laman, 2013; Moll, Saez, & Dworin, 2001; Samway, 2006; Zapata & Laman, 2016). Even though it has been close to 50 years since Graves called upon teachers to shift their thinking about writing, writing instruction is still dominated by programs that steer teachers and children away from authentic writing in favor of writing that is often too formulaic and void of agency and voice. This stance ignores that when children write for meaning, they not only grow as writers, they also meet competencies such as standards.

As researchers have focused on emergent bilingual writers, the following key aspects about the teaching of writing emerge:

- When educators view emergent bilingual students' homes, families, and communities from a perspective of strength (as having a wealth of sociocultural writing resources, funds of knowledge), emergent bilingual children will experience a richer writing environment (D'warte, 2014; Mercado, 2005; Moll et al., 1992). The community literacy practices where the children come from should not only be acknowledged but should also be sustained and built upon (Hudelson, 2000; González et al., 2005).

- When students' spelling and use of language is accepted, and when they can use what they know about writing in their home languages, emergent bilinguals are able to convey complex ideas in writing (Edelsky & Jilbert, 1985; Hudelson, 1989; Serna & Hudelson, 1993).

- When students dialogue with peers in their home languages about their writing and writing process, their capacities as writers improve (Hudelson & Faltis, 1994; Kibler, 2010).

- When bilingual writers compose from a bilingual stance, they show their unique voice as they flexibly use their languages (Fu, 2009). She adds, "Forcing them to think only in English is to cripple the full extent of their intelligence and neglect all their competencies (or funds of knowledge)" (p. 120). García (2009) adds that it also normalizes the language practices of the students' communities.

- We need to pay attention to the purposes of writing (audiences don't come knowing just one language), rather than assuming that the child should only write in English as the ultimate goal (Hudelson & Serna, 1994; Hudelson, 2000). In other words, when children write for authentic audiences, they can write in their home language if that is what the particular audience requires (e.g., an invitation letter to a bilingual play to the parents who speak Spanish).

- To understand the development of bilingual writers and be able to more fully support them, Hudelson (1986) argued that we need to make decisions based on children's work over time, rather than on just one piece of writing.

- We should keep in mind "a vision of the writing process as a way of learning about and making sense of the world and the individual's place in that world, including the possibility of helping to make the world a more equitable place" (Hudelson, 2000 p. 77).

- When students translanguage during writing time, teachers gain insight into their students' lives and can use that insight to teach them in ways that connect more fully to their lives (Ascenzi-Moreno & Espinosa, 2018; Ascenzi-Moreno, 2017; Espinosa, 2006).

A student self-portrait and narrative using translanguaging and multimodality.

- Emergent bilingual children need opportunities to use writing to explore, discover, express themselves, and to think. To do this well, they may need explicit support (Fu, Hadjioannou, & Zhou, 2019).

New Directions for Writing and Emergent Bilinguals

Horner, Lu, Jones, and Trimbur (2011) argue that we must challenge the idea that there is a static and uniform writing standard—a standard that leads to the exclusion and denigration of others' voices and points of view. Instead, these researchers view differences as a resource and as an asset. Another researcher, Canagarajah (2011), adds that by creating this space, the writer's creativity and criticality are nurtured. The writer also has opportunities to re-appropriate and resist traditional, monolingual school discourses, to transcend borders and a rigid separation of languages. Lee and Alvarez (2020) believe that by taking this stance, we begin to dismantle the monolingual ideologies so pervasive in educational institutions. By centering on the languaging practices of emergent bilinguals, Laman and Zapata (2016) argue that emergent bilinguals can engage in deeper thinking and learning. In addition, de los Ríos and Seltzer (2018) propose a framework that views emergent bilinguals as agents and change makers in contesting how they are positioned in the literacy curriculum.

As we review the research from the past and the more current research on writing, we ask, how do we apply a translanguaging lens to writing instruction? How does translanguaging help us make authentic writing experiences available to emergent bilinguals? In this section, we explore, with attention to practices, ways in which emergent bilinguals can actively participate in the writing process.

A Translanguaging Vision for Writing Instruction

Just as we examined reading from a translanguaging perspective, we examine writing from a translanguaging perspective, helping you ensure that writing is an authentic activity that serves as a tool for expanding knowledge and constructing meaning.

We start with core principles about writing for emergent bilinguals. These principles will help you understand writing through a translanguaging lens (Ascenzi-Moreno & Espinosa, 2018, p. 14).

- Writing is writing regardless of the language. Although cultural and language-specific conventions exist, the construction of meaning is at the heart of writing.

- Students need to draw from their entire linguistic repertoire to produce complex texts. To access deeper and more complex thinking, emergent bilinguals need opportunities to enact their agency, rather than solely relying on the teacher to make those choices for them.

- Similarly, students need to draw from their entire linguistic repertoires, regardless of the type of writing they are doing and throughout all aspects of the writing process. This is important, regardless of the language in which the final product is written. Emergent bilinguals benefit from engaging in literacy practices in their home language such as reading, taking notes, conferencing and sharing, and translating, to create a well-crafted final product.

These core principles advocate a translanguaged view of writing and counter-practices that provide emergent bilinguals of all ages with opportunities to engage in authentic and expansive writing experiences at all times. It is critical that these experiences are developmentally appropriate and are culturally and linguistically sustaining.

Into the Classroom
Writing That Is Connected to the World

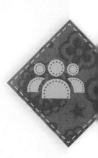

In this Into the Classroom, we share short vignettes across three grades to demonstrate how translanguaging in writing can be carried out in different ways.

Kindergarten

"¡Buenos días, niños!" announces Ms. Corral, a kindergarten teacher in an early-exit bilingual class. "Today we are going to take a walking trip for our community study. What do you think you may see?" Ms. Corral takes dictation as the children call out what they think they may see.

> La tienda de la esquina
>
> The crossing guard
>
> La entrada al park
>
> The entrance to the park
>
> La gente con sus dogs
>
> People with their dogs

After Ms. Corral reads the list with the class, she asks a few children to translate some of the words for the English speakers and the Spanish speakers. Ms. Corral accepts the children's sentence "la gente con sus dogs" and writes it as the child said it. In reading the sentence to the class, she reads it as the child dictated it to her. She also provides the word for *dogs* in Spanish, *perros*. She helps the children notice the cognates "park/parque" and "guard/guardia." She writes the letters that are the same in one color and the letters that are different in another.

When the class returns from the community walk, Ms. Corral shares some photographs she took, and the children add to the list. You can see how she capitalized fully on the children's linguistic repertoires to help them construct meaning.

Second Grade

In Mr. Duarte's dual-language bilingual class, a team of four students is in charge of writing about their trip to the zoo for a family newsletter. Spanish is the home language of two of those students. Mr. Duarte reminds the children that some of the parents speak Spanish. So, he asks them to write a brief description of their trip to the zoo in English and Spanish. Mr. Duarte provides the children with tablets so, as they write, they can use an electronic dictionary or thesaurus if they need to look up words.

Third Grade

In Ms. Torres's general education classroom, students are writing personal narratives. Ms. Torres tells them that when her mother talks to her, it is usually in Spanish. So, when she models how to write dialogue, she composes most of the text in English, except for when her mom talks. Then she uses Spanish. Ms. Torres shows the students a book by Gary Soto, *Too Many Tamales* (1996), in which the characters translanguage, which is typical in Soto's books. They study select passages and talk about ways they can draw from their own lives and languages when they write.

As you can see in these examples, there are many ways to capitalize on students' resources through translanguaging. When planning a writing exercise, ask yourself, "How can I ensure that the children are constructing meaning through translanguaging? What happens when everyone has an opportunity to use their full linguistic repertoire?"

The Writing Environment From a Translanguaging Stance

As with reading, setting up a writing environment where multilingualism is the norm is critical. When we refer to the writing environment, we refer not only to the physical environment, which is important, but also the practices that create a multilingual writing community, including our own writing practices.

The Physical Environment

Consider the physical environment you create to support students. One of the first steps is to ensure that students have resources that reflect their multilingualism. Similar to the reading environment, the writing environment should contain print around the room, such as posters, anchor charts, and children's own writing, as well as accessible references (e.g., dictionaries, thesaurus), student-made dictionaries, including digital references (e.g., a translation app on an iPad), and other writing tools. The classroom should offer examples of writing that exist in the real world, including children's communities, in the languages they speak. This may include fiction and nonfiction texts, environmental print, songs, poems, magazines, newspapers, and student- and teacher-made announcements. Also consider tools that allow the students to access words in other languages (e.g., digital and print dictionaries and thesauruses).

A student created an Arabic-English picture dictionary.

Lastly, as we mentioned earlier, it is important to understand children's home literacies—and connect to their funds of knowledge. Perhaps you can find a neighborhood newspaper written in their home language, or an example of an email or note written by a parent, or a newsletter prepared by the principal. Perhaps your class can write a newsletter for families in the languages those families speak. All of these examples show children how multilingual writing exists in the world. They show that writing has a purpose and a function, and that writers write with an audience in mind. In fact, figuring out that writing is purposeful is the most important discovery a young child can make.

Here are some ideas for creating a multilingual writing landscape:

Second-grade teacher Rebecca Quiñones provides students with resources in Spanish and English for writing.

- In your community, take photographs of print in different languages. Make sure you talk with the children about the photos.

- Display children's writing in languages they and their families speak.

- Create charts with the children in languages that the children and their families speak.

- Acquire diverse books in various genres that the class can use as mentor texts (poetry, nonfiction, biography, narratives, etc). that represent the named language backgrounds of the students.

- Refresh books in the classroom library regularly to reflect children's identities and language backgrounds.

It's important to consider how you can set up a community of writers that welcomes and values translanguaging. We recommend that one of your first whole-class meetings focuses on the idea of multilingualism. During that meeting, you can share how writers use all the resources they have to ensure their writing makes sense, regardless of the language in which they're writing. You can also highlight ways writers use multilingual voices.

You should also think about who sits next to whom during mini-lessons and independent writing time so that students can serve as language resources for each other. After all, in a true community of writers, each child has something to say and knows that what he or she has to say will be heard (Laman, 2013). By listening carefully to classmates' oral and written stories, messages, nonfiction texts, and poems, students learn how to be attentive audience members who help the writer figure out what the reader needs from him or her, what is missing, and what is clear. Writing instruction becomes student-centered, rather than teacher-centered.

In Chapter 2, we invited you to examine who the children in your class are, the languages they speak, and the resources that they bring to school. Use what you gained from that exercise to think about your students as writers from a perspective of strength. The following questions will help:

- What do I know about the emergent bilingual children in my class as writers?
- What writing experiences do the emergent bilingual children have?
- What do my students understand about writing?
- Are there opportunities for my students to pursue their interests through writing?
- Are there multimodal opportunities for my students to create texts?
- What motivates my students to write?
- Do I offer opportunities for emergent bilingual children to write collaboratively?
- Am I modeling how I capitalize on my entire linguistic repertoire to support my writing?
- What tools are available for students to support their writing?
- What experiences can they draw from when choosing topics of writing?

Routines and Expectations

As we stated with regard to reading, if your schedule is predictable, your routines and expectations clear, and your instruction student-centered, emergent bilingual children will take ownership and fully exercise their agency during writing time. Think carefully about your vision for that time. To support children's writing development, create charts with them on topics such as routines for writing, how writers get ideas, and what writers do when they don't know how to spell a word. In the process, you will be modeling how to draft, organize ideas, and make the ideas inviting. In other words, you will be making explicit your thinking process as a writer. You will also be sending a message that, in the real world, writers put a lot of thought into their writing, and that their writing has a purpose.

The routines you establish during writing time need to be inclusive of the children's linguistic backgrounds. Remember, just like reading, writing is writing regardless of the languages in which it is done.

The following questions will help you reflect on the way you set up the writing time and create routines and expectations:

- How will I organize the writing time so that routines are consistent, and the children know when it happens and how it happens?

- What is my role in supporting all of my students as they write and learn about language?

- What do I know about how emergent bilingual students write, and, based on that understanding, how can I support them as they write?

- What do I know about the writing practices of students' families?

- What will I share with emergent bilingual students about what I value about writing and the practices I want them to develop?

- In what ways do those practices contribute to, sustain, and celebrate the children's multilingualism?

- How do I invite children to access their entire linguistic repertoires as they write? What structures do I have in place to ensure that students can access those resources?

Action 10

Reflect on Your Relationship to Writing

Our practices are shaped by our beliefs. When we reflect upon our personal histories with writing, how we were taught to teach writing, and how we currently teach writing, we are better able to understand how our mindsets impact our practice.

In this Action, we ask you to reflect on your writing history and then to consider, based on your thoughts, how you want your work with emergent bilinguals to take shape.

1. Answer each of the following questions in writing.

   - What does writing mean to me?

   - How did I learn to write?

   - When has writing come easily for me? When hasn't it?

   - What is my experience writing in a different language?

   - What support would I need to learn to write in a new language?

   - What does it mean for me to capitalize on my entire linguistic repertoire when I write?

2. Based on your answers, what is your vision for developing writers in your classroom, including emergent bilinguals? What support do you need to realize your vision? What needs to change?

Closing Thoughts

We must eliminate the deficit perspective for emergent bilingual writers—the idea that they cannot become true writers until they have enough English language to participate in authentic writing experiences. We advocate for multilingual writing environments that provide students with opportunities to engage in a writerly life, using all of their language resources. You can support emergent bilinguals as writers by reflecting on yourself as a writer and the writing environment that supports and values multilingualism.

Suggestions for Professional Development

In this section, you will be asked to reflect on your own writing process, as well as write from a translanguaging perspective. You will also be asked to consider the writing environment you envision for emergent bilinguals.

1 Respond to Chapter 1 from *Merci Suárez Changes Gears* (2018) by Meg Medina. After reading the short story or hearing it read out loud, write a letter to one of the characters. For the purposes of this experience, we are asking you to write it twice. The first time, write the letter to one of the characters in a named language that is new to you. (In other words, don't use a translation tool, and don't rely on a colleague to translate for you.) In a small group, spend a few minutes debriefing what this experience was like for you as a writer. What was it like to write a letter in this way without being able to draw on your entire linguistic repertoire?

2 For the second letter you write to one of the characters, use your entire linguistic repertoire. Once you have written the letter, share it with the same small group of colleagues. In addition, share what you experienced as a writer when you could capitalize on your entire linguistic repertoire. Compare it to what happened when you could only use your new language. Spend a few minutes debriefing what this experience was like for you as a writer.

3 Take a few minutes to respond in small groups to the questions in Action 10. Share your responses about your vision for teaching emergent bilinguals to write, given your experiences. What changes could you pinpoint to support emergent bilinguals as writers as a result of this discussion?

4 Consider how you can organize the writing time in a small group so that the daily routines are consistent. Choose two or three of the questions on page 152 and bring your responses to the group. After the discussion, think about some new multilingual practices you can incorporate and which ones you want to know more about.

Questions about your students' and their families' writing practices	What do you currently know or do?	What are some new multilingual practices you can incorporate? Which ones do you want to know more about?
How do you want to organize the writing time so that it is consistent (e.g., the children know it always happens and how it happens)?		
What is your role as a teacher in supporting all of your students as they write and learn language?		
What do you know about how your emergent bilingual students write? Based on this understanding, how can you support them as they write?		
What do you know about your students' families' writing practices outside of school?		
What valuable writing practices do you want to share with emergent bilinguals in your class?		
How do you ensure there are structures in place for the children to access their entire linguistic repertoires as they write? How do you ensure access?		

CHAPTER 8

The Beginnings of Writing

"What is needed to support young emergent bilingual writers? A vision of writing as a way of learning about and making sense of the world and the individual's place in that world, including the possibility of helping to make the world a more equitable place."

—SARAH HUDELSON

Children are interested in writing even before they enter school. As they observe their family members writing at home, children intuitively understand that writing has purpose. After all, their parents never just practice writing; they use writing to accomplish a wide range of purposes. Writing, like talking, is language (K. Goodman & Y. Goodman, 2014)—and all language is functional; indeed, it's easier to learn language when we have a real reason to use it. Most children grow up immersed in print. Outside the home, this includes environmental print such as road signs, billboards, commercial signage, and product labels. Inside their homes, children encounter print on television and the Internet, and in the print that arrives daily, such as the mail, newspapers, and magazines. Additionally, much of this print is multimodal. Children interact with text through song lyrics, religious activities, cooking, baking, and just being in the world.

When children are learning to speak, we always assume that they are using language to express themselves and communicate their needs. We treat their intentions as meaningful and purposeful. We don't wait for children to speak in complete, grammatically correct sentences before we're willing to interpret their desires, intentions, and purposes. A very young child might say, for example, "Da, eche." The intended message might be, "Papá, quiero más leche [Daddy, I want more milk.]." The parent does not respond, "I will give you milk when you deliver a complete sentence in English. You need to practice your oral communication!" Rather, the parent responds to the meaning of the child's expression: "I see you are hungry. Let me get you some leche, aquí está tu leche" or perhaps a question, "¿Tienes hambre? ¡Wow! ¡La leche está muy rica!" (adding to the conversation).

Writing is language, just like talking is language. As we stated earlier, at the core of writing is also the construction of meaning (Berthoff, 1981; Hudelson, 2000, 2005; Espinosa, Ascenzi-Moreno, & Vogel, 2016; 2020). Even the smallest mark a child makes on a page holds meaning (the maker's intention). Therefore, how the adult responds to the child's intentions to support young children's oral language development, and later writing, matters. The child learns early on that writing has a purpose, that it holds social significance, based on how others respond to the child's intentions.

Writing is active; it serves innumerable purposes in the world. Authentic writing is not "filling in the blanks," as students are often asked to do in school. Samway (2006) writes, "When I refer to *writing*, I am thinking of the creation of an original text, no matter how complex or simple the message. I am not referring to the copying of sentences, the making of sentences from a word list, or filling in blanks, which often comprise the school writing experiences of many students, particularly young children and English language learners" (p. 22).

As in oral language, children make approximations when they are learning to write. The term *invented spelling* was coined by researcher Charles Read in 1986. He stated that children's invented spellings show us what the child knows about writing (that it conveys an intended message, that sounds represent letters, that there is a space between words, that there are punctuation marks, etc.). Children who are writing a book, for example, using invented spelling and drawings, are already engaged in the complex process of composing (Wood Ray, 2008). Not only are the children learning to fill the pages with their intended message, but they are also figuring out their genre—fiction, nonfiction, poetry, personal narrative, or perhaps a combination. As the children move from page to page, they discover what they want to say. Once finished, the children might share their books with an audience and learn that they can talk to others about their writing. The process of learning to write conventionally takes many years. Learning to write well—in a way that conveys the writer's voice, perspective, and ideas with clarity— is a lifelong journey.

How Does Writing Begin?

Children's early writing often appears as a combination of scribbles and drawings. Eventually, children attempt to make letters—often representing the letters in their own name—and use them in ways that reflect their understanding of letter/sound relationships. With the help of adults, they may begin to explore other words that hold particular importance, such as *mamá* and *papá*. For emergent bilingual children, these words might be related to their own home or community.

In the midst of learning about writing through their own exploration, children are also learning to manipulate writing tools and to control the marks they can make on the page (lines, circles, dots, etc.). Once children enter school, the teacher helps them notice the unique differences among all the letters of the alphabet—for example, how the letter *M* is formed, or the different lines that comprise the letter *B*. The teacher provides daily demonstrations of letter-making, talking about each letter's different sounds and shapes. The purpose is not to drill the children but to support their natural interest in letters, sounds, and writing. While handwriting instruction may be helpful for school-age children, very young children do not have the muscle control for "official" handwriting instruction.

Children also learn to organize print on the page—writing from top to bottom, and in many languages, left to right. And once children develop an understanding of "wordness," they begin to add spaces between each word they write, which is a more challenging writing convention for many children. As children learn to write, they are also figuring out how their language works. Initially, children cannot hear all the phonemes (the smallest units of sound) in words; for example, they might spell the word *love* with just two letters, *lv*. At this point, the adult can provide support in "sounding out" the word—stretching it out like a rubber band or sliding through the letters and emphasizing each individual phoneme—so the child can begin to learn the conventional spelling.

The role of the adult, parent, or teacher is to meet children where they are, developmentally—and, building on what they can already do, help them develop new understandings and skills. Also, parents and teachers can reassure children not to worry about so-called mistakes but to take the risks necessary to learn. In this way, with each interaction with print, children receive new opportunities for learning. When children are invited to take learning risks, their writing becomes more complex. They feel free to explore all aspects of written language—new genres, punctuation, sentence structures—rather than perfectly spelled words in a series of repetitive, patterned sentences such as: *I like dogs. I like horses. I like cats.* Learning to write is a complex orchestration of multiple understandings about written language and how it works (Freeman & Freeman, 2009). Children learn to control writing on a global level—to express themselves and communicate with others—as well as on a particular level—how letters, sounds, and words work together to create a meaningful message.

The Role of Responsive Teaching

A question Marie Clay (1975) posed many years ago still resonates: How can teachers sharpen their observation of children's efforts? She challenged the field to thoughtfully consider the questions that arise when we study and examine children's emergent writing. Clay argued early on in her research that children don't learn to write in a particular adult-imposed sequence: learning the letters of the alphabet first, then words, then sentences. While this might make teaching easier, it's not the meaning-driven, natural way children learn. Clay argues that children learn about writing as they explore all these different levels simultaneously.

Years ago, in his seminal text *Writing: Teachers and Children at Work* (1983), Donald Graves also made clear that a young child does not need to know all the letters of the alphabet in order to create a message that conveys meaning. At first, the child may only know the letters of her name. She might rearrange these letters to convey a message filled with strings of letters used in a repetitive manner. Over time, she will learn about the directionality of written language. In alphabetic languages such as English and Spanish, writing starts at the top (left). The writer moves from left to right, returns back to the left side, and again moves toward the right. Children benefit immeasurably when they have access to an adult who supports their developmental writing process—which includes, in part, figuring out the alphabetic system while sustaining the important idea that at the core of writing is the construction of meaning.

The act of writing is hard work, involving thought and the complex orchestration of many aspects of language. As we discussed earlier, the writing process is not linear (pre-writing, writing, rewriting), nor does it necessarily begin with or follow an outline. Often writers do not know what exactly they are going to write—until they begin writing. Janet Emig's (1971) research demonstrated that, as writers compose, they often go back and forth between the text and their thoughts. Writing, she argued, is a complex, recursive process. Additionally, writing can help the writer to explore, to rethink, and to further understand an idea. Samway (2006) notes, "in fact, through writing, we discover what we think and know" (p. 7). She adds, "when we write, we embark on a process that allows us to discover what we want to write about…" (p. 8). All of this makes the writing process a personal journey, rather than a series of linear and sequential steps. Thus, while writers may plan, draft, and revise their writing, they may not engage in these steps in a particular sequence.

Practical Ways to Demonstrate Writing and Engage Beginning Writers

"What a child can do with assistance today, she will be able to do by herself tomorrow."

—LEV VYGOTSKY

Oral language is the gateway to literacy (Velasco & Espinosa, forthcoming). Our knowledge of language begins as we use language to communicate with others—through listening and participating in conversations. We learn language throughout our lives. Writing for our youngest students begins through talk (Gort, 2012). Students play with language and ideas as they generate topics to write and draw about. This often occurs in the company of other children. For emergent bilingual students, playing with language as a stage in pre-writing occurs fluidly between both languages (Gort, 2012). Therefore, writing instruction for young emergent bilinguals must be supported with ample opportunities—both planned and unplanned—for multilingual talk. This can take shape through turn and talks, writing with partners, and free talk while writing.

The Language Experience Approach

From a translanguaging perspective, the Language Experience Approach integrates the child's entire linguistic repertoire through all components of language: listening, speaking, reading, and writing. Together, the students and teacher generate a text that is often based on a shared experience. They begin by discussing the experience—a field trip, a classroom visitor, someone's birthday, and so forth. The teacher invites the children to use the full range of their linguistic repertoires to talk about the experience, strategically pairing children by language, for example. Once the children and the teacher have an opportunity to discuss the experience, the teacher explains that next, the children will take turns dictating to the teacher their ideas about what to write about their shared experience (Dorr, 2006). As the children suggest sentences and words that capture the experience, the teacher demonstrates her writing moves—for example, how to orient the print from left to right, top to bottom; how to start a personal name with a capital letter, how to spell *mother*, which includes the "th" sound; how to use a capital letter after a period.

When utilizing the language experience approach, the teacher is working with vocabulary the children know and use. It is often the case that when a text comprises words the children have generated, it is easier for them to read. This is why it is important that we invite children to use their entire linguistic repertoires. At times, this may look like using words from different named languages in one text. Once the text is written, the class can read it together. The teacher can point to words, helping the children make letter-sound correspondence connections, notice the spacing between words, as well as make predictions about what the next letters and sounds, words, phrases, or sentences will be, with a focus on meaning (e.g., what letters come after *moth* when writing the word *mother*). Ideally, the teacher will send the text home as a reading assignment, *asking* the children to read the text to their families at home. This way, the experience and the text can be revisited with an authentic audience and is meaningful to the children.

Interactive Writing

Interactive writing is another collaborative writing experience in which you can engage your emergent bilingual students. As the child holds the marker, you help him or her think about what to write and how to write it. You might ask a child to come up to the board to write an entire word, a phrase, or just a letter. You can weave interactive writing into your daily routines. For example, you can invite children to write a class message. The purpose is to make explicit

Into the Classroom

The Language Experience Approach— How Is It Done?

In Karina's second-grade bilingual class, the children have returned from a field trip to the zoo. Since there is still an hour of school before going home, she invites them to the carpet. She asks them to turn to a partner and share something about their experience at the zoo. She has strategically partnered the children in her class, according to shared linguistic repertoires. She invites them to use all of their linguistic resources when they share with each other. Next, Karina takes a few minutes to engage the children in a conversation about the zoo experience. She explains that they are going to write an announcement that they can take home to read to their families about their trip to the zoo. She asks the children to share some ideas that they might want to share with their parents. A few partners are speaking in Spanish. As the children share, Karina acts as the scribe—writing down the children's dialogue. She slows down her writing in order to make her

thinking visible. When a child shares in a language other than English, Karina asks another child to share the message in English. As she rereads out loud what has been written, she talks about punctuation, focusing on capital letters and periods. After the children finish dictating the message, Karina reads it to the class and invites the children to join in with her.

The next day, Karina types the message the children co-wrote with her. It goes home as part of the reading assignments. She asks the children to read it to at least two family members. The Language Experience Approach is a perfect partner for translanguaging. The teacher invites students to speak in any language and may also pose inquiries, such as, "How do you say tiger in the languages you speak?". This conversation opens up a space for students to be curious about language and to feel comfortable sharing and hearing all of the languages represented in the classroom.

to everyone in the class how writing works while giving a few children the opportunity to come up in front to write in a very supportive environment (Roth & Dabrowski, 2016). The aim is to prepare an interactive writing lesson that meets the emergent bilingual children where they are, while also challenging them to gain new insights about writing. During interactive writing, encourage students to speak about the similarities and differences between the sounds of letters of the languages that they know. This type of talk during interactive writing is helpful for building metacognitive awareness. It is also a time that students can talk about the words that they know across languages by talking with others about the things and experiences that are important to them.

Shared Writing

Shared writing offers you the opportunity to explicitly demonstrate writing to a whole group or a small group of children, while meeting them within their zone of proximal development (Vygotsky, 1978). It is also an occasion for children and teachers to collaboratively compose a text. You might choose to demonstrate for the children a pattern of spelling, punctuation, dialogue, a detailed description, or even how to expand a sentence or write a letter (Routman, 2005). You might also engage the children in making connections across languages to help them develop their language awareness. Just as children explore and develop their language and meta-language experience in interactive writing, this is a space for students to develop their language awareness in early childhood across the languages that they know. During group literacy experiences like shared writing, the class community can talk about different words that mean the same thing (e.g., *bag, funda, bolsa*), the different sounds of their languages, and their different experiences. Immersing the class in this rich dialogue contributes to the normality of

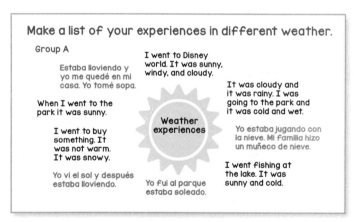

Kindergarten dual-language bilingual teachers take dictation to create a shared writing experience with their students using translanguaging.

multilingualism and helps students understand that language diversity is not only normal, but also fascinating and exciting!

Writing lessons emerge from your careful observations of the students' writing and talk about text, including texts written by the students, as well as texts from the classroom library. After your explicit shared writing demonstration, the children should discuss what they have learned and try it out themselves during independent writing time.

Into the Classroom

Interactive Writing—How Is It Done?

In Ms. Lugo's kindergarten class, the children are composing the message of the day. Usually Ms. Lugo writes the message for the children. She writes the beginning of the message as she always does, "Today is ..." The children talk about the date and she writes the complete date. Next, they talk about something special that will happen on this day. She tells them, "We have music." She invites a child to come to the board, hold the pen, and write the word *We*. She invites the class to help sound out the word. They continue with the word *have*. She invites a couple more children to write this word. The teacher stretches the word, so the children can hear and experience how it is written. She talks about the silent *e* in *have*. She takes this opportunity to explain to the children that in Spanish the letter *e* always has the same sound, while in English, in some words, it remains silent; it does not make a sound. When they get to the word *music*, she asks the children what the translation of the word *music* in Spanish is. A child replies *música*. Ms. Lugo writes *música* at the top of the chart paper where they are writing the sentence. She calls on a child to write the word *music*. The rest of the class and Ms. Lugo help the child by stretching out the word and sounding out each sound they hear. Once it is written, Ms. Lugo asks them to compare the spelling. She asks them, "What do you notice about the words *music* and *música*?" Ms. Lugo explains that when two words in two different languages are spelled similarly, they are called *cognates*. She adds that they will start a chart on the wall where they can collect these words. The class continues by talking about the period that goes at the end of the sentence. Once they have completed the writing, the class reads the message together.

Into the Classroom

Shared Writing—How Is It Done?

Karina decided to create a shared writing lesson in order to support her second-grade students' metalinguistic awareness across languages. In this lesson, she explains that diminutives in English are constructed differently from diminutives in Spanish. She uses the song "los pollitos dicen pío, pío, pío..." to help the children notice how one might write a diminutive in Spanish, "ito." As the children sing the song, Karina points to the words of the song which she has written on chart paper, noting that in Spanish, "ito" is used to refer to something small and little. She calls on a few children to help her say the diminutive of other animals and write *perro, gato, pato*. Then she asks her Spanish speakers to help her say the diminutive of each animal. The children share *perrito, gatito*, and *patito*. She then writes next to each word and underlines the "ito" that turns the word into a diminutive.

perro—perrito

gato—gatito

pato—patito

Next, she writes the words in English. She asks the children to think about how people might do the same thing in English; in other words, talk about a cute, little animal. The children help her by dictating the following:

dog—doggy

cat—kitty

duck—ducky

Karina closes the lesson by reminding the children how important it is that they study similarities and differences across languages because it helps them understand more about each language.

Writing Workshop:
A Way to Organize Writing Time

The advantage of the writing workshop is that it provides students with a consistent space in which to develop their writing through a structure that teachers provide. However, in our experience, when we taught writing, the curriculum that we used was based solely on two modalities of writing—speaking and writing. For emergent bilinguals, all four modalities of language are important— talking, writing, listening, and reading. Our students are dynamic beings and experience the world through dancing, running, playing, moving, eating, and so on. Writing should be a reflection of life. The inner lives of children and the writing process could be enhanced for all children— including emergent bilinguals—through the inclusion of multimodal ways of entering into the writing process. This includes writing about shared experiences, incorporating drama and art to add details. Think about how writing time is organized in your class and how it evokes students' diverse experiences to harness their multilingual and multimodal resources.

Our students are dynamic beings and experience the world through dancing, running, playing, moving, eating, and so on. Writing should be a reflection of life.

How Does Your Writing Time Support Emergent Bilingual Students?

Teachers organize their writing time in different ways. Some have the agency to structure writing time in ways that work best for themselves and their students. Other times, the school mandates a particular structure. We think it is important for you, the teacher, to have a say about the way in which writing is taught in your school. An essential element of the writing workshop, regardless of structure, is consistent, dedicated time daily to grow as writers. For both of us, the schedule of a "writing workshop" with the structure described in this chapter has worked. As we describe the structure, we will also point out how emergent bilinguals may be supported throughout each of these familiar writing workshop structures.

Mini-Lessons

Mini-lessons, which typically take place at the beginning of the workshop, are the heart of the writing process. While they are short—approximately 10 minutes—much is done during the mini-lesson for writers, in general, and also for emergent bilingual writers. The goals of the mini-lesson include:

- to communicate the instructional challenge—a skill or task they might face as writers
- to model how the teacher would address this task
- to provide students with structured time so they can practice the task with partners

One of the challenges that emergent bilinguals may face during this time is that often all of the information may be presented solely in one language. To address this concern, you might think about how you can make your mini-lesson more multilingual and multimodal.

Mini-lessons often start with a whole group. You might want to make sure that partners are sitting strategically. Perhaps ask the children to sit next to a bilingual child or two; partners who speak the same language can sit next to each other. Maybe ask a child to translate portions (not the entire lesson) for the other children. (Translation requires high-order thinking, just like paraphrasing does, so by no means is it an inferior use of time.)

How you use the few minutes of the mini-lesson matters. The topics at the heart of the mini-lesson can bring students' multilingual strengths to the forefront. Here are some ways to do that:

- Talk about what it means to be a community of writers who translanguage.
- Talk about the characteristics of a particular genre (e.g., narratives often have dialogue). When the characters are bilingual, the authors often make it authentic by making sure the dialogue reflects the characters' ability to speak two languages.
- Examine the structure of a piece of writing. Look at a story, a poem, or a nonfiction text and examine how the author constructed it. Invite the children to share their thinking using their linguistic resources.

- Listen to a piece of music and talk about how the music may be related to an important feeling to include in their writing.

- Examine illustrations in a book and talk about how they add to the story.

- Ask the children to share what they notice, using all their language practices.

- Study the reasons why a beloved classroom author writes and what connections that piece has to the author's life. Study, for example, the work of bilingual authors, such as Jen Arena, Juan Felipe Herrera, Juana Medina, Pat Mora, or Emma Otheguy.

- Use a mentor text, a text that teachers and students often return to, to show a crafting technique (e.g., authentic dialogue in other languages, how authors begin a text, how authors show, not tell, etc.).

- Use drama to understand how authors craft a scene. While engaging the children in drama, invite them to think about the nuances of word meanings (e.g., what does *mad* look like and feel like in the body, and what gestures would you use to convey *mad*?) Look for the meaning of the word in children's languages other than English. For example, ask students to dramatize the word *enojado*.

- Compose a class piece together that involves translanguaging. The children can tell you what to write in the language other than English. Demonstrate whether you need to translate it into English, based on who your audience is.

- Let the children see your thinking as a bilingual writer.

Keep your mini-lesson focused on the one idea that you are teaching while you are capitalizing on the children's entire linguistic repertoires. In this way, you ensure that you provide students with ample ways to understand and engage in the mini-lesson.

Action 11

Infuse Your Mini-Lessons With Multilingualism

In Action 11, we ask you to think about the mini-lesson in multilingual ways. First, think about the text you will use to engage students. Can you use books that are reflective of students' identities (España & Herrera, 2020; Pérez, 2015)? Consider how you may engage the students. Consider the language you use when you explain the objective of the lesson. If you are a bilingual teacher, you may be able to use English and another language. If you teach in a monolingual setting, think about how you could either use key words in more than one language, translate parts of the connection, or ask students to assist in translating portions of a part of the mini-lesson.

Next, engage in a demonstration to show students how writers face a particular challenge. Think aloud and/or compose in front of the children so that students can gain an understanding of how experienced writers engage in writing. If you are a bilingual teacher, how will you demonstrate how you make meaning while you write? This can be done by doing a think-aloud in one language and then writing in another. You could draw from your full linguistic repertoire to write. If you are a monolingual teacher, you can ask students to watch your demonstration, but also ask students to think and discuss your model using their own home languages, as would be helpful.

The space for active engagement provides ample opportunities for students to engage their full linguistic repertoires. When you pair students, you can think about their language resources that will affect talk partnerships. You may choose to have students who speak the same language other than English together for one activity and then to have students from two different language backgrounds paired together for another part of the activity. Student partnerships also provide the perfect opportunity to infuse multimodality into the lesson—for example, students can talk to each other, but they can also act out a part.

You can remind the students that when they are working independently, they can engage in translanguaging in multiple ways: by talking to others before, during, or after writing, or even by using translanguaging in a piece itself. When you are conferencing with students, you can document, encourage, and support students' translanguaging to move their writing forward.

Lastly, don't forget to consider that when it's time to gather students for a whole-group share—another venue for welcoming a translanguaging space—students can share their work, addressing how they used their entire linguistic repertoires. They can also share texts that include translanguaging.

Writing Conferences

During writing conferences with emergent bilinguals, make sure that children feel they have agency to draw on their linguistic resources to support their writing. Meet with the child for about 10 minutes while the rest of the children work independently. Since writing conferences are also a form of assessment, you can find out more about how conferences can contribute to informal assessment while supporting individual writers in Chapter 10.

Peer Conferences

Conferences can happen between children. While children can conference with one another through each stage of the writing process, "receiving the piece" is a powerful way for children to provide feedback to one another. It helps children learn to listen fully to one another's stories. To ensure success, Ms. Albert used a "fish bowl" technique with Eliana to demonstrate how to receive the piece.

Ms. Albert says, "I need everybody to sit in a circle. Eliana and I will be sitting in these chairs side by side. In this class, we always talk about helping each other with our writing. I am going to show you a new process. It is called 'receiving the piece.' Can someone please translate what I just said? Receiving the piece asks that you listen very carefully to your partner." [She points to her ear.] "I have you set up as partners. I will be telling you later who you will be working with. When you are receiving the piece, it is very important that you listen with your heart, your mind, and your body. So how we sit facing each other is important. Eliana, ¿puedes sentarte aquí frente a mí? Eliana me va a contar su historia."

Eliana shares her story in Spanish.

Ms. Albert listens attentively. She repeats the story in Spanish to Eliana, and then asks another child to translate it into English for the class.

Ms. Albert asks Eliana questions about the story in order to support Eliana in more fully telling her story. "What were you and your grandma cooking?"

Now it is Eliana's turn to receive the piece from Ms. Albert.

Next, Ms. Albert asks the children to practice the strategy of receiving the piece. Ms. Albert has organized the partners by language. This way the children will have both freedom and support to use their entire linguistic repertoires.

Below are the steps for the process of receiving the piece that you can put in place to support the conferences among children.

Receiving the Piece

The primary purpose of receiving the piece is to show writers what they already know and to gain a clearer picture of what they will write next. Strategically partner students so they can share, using their entire linguistic repertoires. Partners work together; the first one reads/talks about his or her piece, and the other one receives it. Then the roles are reversed.

1. The writer begins by telling the listener what the piece is about.
2. The writer chooses to either orally read or tell the whole story to the listener.
3. The listener pays close attention.
4. The listener retells the story back to the writer, using as many of the actual words the writer used as possible.
5. The listener makes comments regarding connections he or she made while listening to the piece and what was particularly striking about the piece. Remind students that it is okay to make these comments using their entire linguistic repertoires.
6. The listener can ask one or two questions to learn more about the piece.
7. The writer replies to the questions the listener posed.
8. The writer and listener switch roles and repeat the process.

Adapted for emergent bilingual students from Graves, 1983; Fletcher, 2017.

Sharing

The last few minutes of writing time should be dedicated to children sharing their work. At times you will want to have a whole-group meeting, where you select particular children to share their writing because of the interesting work you noticed them doing. Perhaps a child used translanguaging in the dialogue about a story, and you want to help the class think further about this possibility. At other times, you might organize small groups of four to five children so that everyone gets a chance to share. The tone you set during sharing time is critical. Sharing time should be a time for children to think about writing and respond to the writer from a writer's perspective, such as, "I like how your illustrations match what you wrote in each page of your book." And always, make sure the children know that they can use their full spectrum of language resources. You might offer the children the following language stems to support the children's responses. All of these language stems could be offered in all the named languages children use.

- Something that I noticed about writing is…
- I did not understand when…
- I like how you…
- It reminds me of…
- I think you should…
- Could you tell me more about…

Publication and Writing Celebration

A few times a year, set aside time to celebrate your young writers and their writing. While celebrations can include children's families, other students, and members of the community, we suggest that your first celebration be just for the children in your class. Consider scheduling it early in the year so that your students quickly learn what it means to take writing from its inception to a published piece. Comments can be limited to a "thank you" or "gracias" to the writer. Once again, emphasize the importance of students listening with their whole bodies, hearts, and minds. Later, when you include others in your celebrations, offer guidelines so that family and community members are not mere spectators, but truly contribute to the conversations and enjoyment of their children as writers.

In the next chapter, we include writing techniques, tools, and possibilities that you can integrate into your writing workshop. These engagements are meant to enhance your repertoire of writing instruction. They are meant to provide entry points where students can begin to weave in both their linguistic and social repertoires in creative and meaningful ways.

Closing Thoughts

In this chapter, we explained that writing for young emergent bilinguals does not always follow a linear path. Instead, it is rooted in multilingual practices that are contextualized in family and community practices. Teachers can support this process by honoring and building on the resources that students bring to school. We stress that writing is a recursive process that is a mix of scaffolded instruction, discovery, and determination. Writing for emergent bilinguals is supported by building on other modalities such as oral language, listening, and reading. Teachers are able to provide opportunities through instructional spaces, such as language experience, shared writing, and mini-lessons, to build on students' multilingual resources to become strong writers.

Suggestions for Professional Development

Continue to think about writing development for emergent bilingual children. We will ask you to try out the language experience approach, interactive writing, and mini-lessons.

1 Gather writing samples every month from one of your young emergent bilinguals. If you are working with a colleague or two, put these samples alongside each other, not to evaluate the students' growth, but to notice across the samples how writing develops for your young emergent bilinguals. What do you notice about how they engage in drawing and writing? How are their families and communities represented? In what ways is the child drawing on the family's and community's funds of knowledge? What implications does this have for you as their teacher of writing? What mini-lessons would you develop? What changes would you make to your writing time?

2 Plan with a colleague a language experience appropriate for your grade level, keeping in mind the emergent bilingual children in your class. Think about how the language experience may be connected to what your class is studying. Also consider how the language experience activity that your plan is connected to can extend students' knowledge. Think about how children may connect to the experience and how it will engage them. Also consider the language that you may want to highlight and what kinds of open-ended questions you may want to ask as a way to help your students engage with their full linguistic repertoires. Share your activity with your colleagues for comments. Colleagues could provide feedback on what they think would work well and how to further deepen ways to support language growth.

3 Invite colleagues to observe as you engage a small group or a class in interactive writing. Have them look for how you engage your students' full linguistic repertoires during the interactive lesson, how students talk to you and one another, and what knowledge of language they draw from. Additionally, ask your colleagues to keep track of the translanguaging opportunities that were present during the lesson and offer ideas for what you could do in the future to provide additional opportunities.

4 Video record the mini-lesson you design after engaging in Action 11. You can choose to view this recording alone for personal reflection or with colleagues. Reflect on student engagement during your mini-lesson. Did all students participate? How did they engage using their full linguistic repertoires? How did you provide entry points for students' translanguaging? How did your scaffolding support student engagement and learning throughout the lesson?

CHAPTER 9

Writing Techniques, Tools, and Possibilities

"An alternative writing world is one where students experience and learn about writing and other possibilities for their writing beyond essays and written responses that have become normalized teaching and learning practices ... writing, even for academic purposes, can be personal, creative, and powerful."

—LATRISE P. JOHNSON

For writing spaces to be engaging and powerful, young emergent bilingual writers need access to a variety of tools, including multimodal tools that can help them use writing to think, reflect, communicate, wonder, and imagine. Young emergent bilingual writers also need opportunities to apprentice from other authors' writing techniques, by trying them out in their own writing. Teaching young emergent bilinguals how to envision themselves as writers who write with purpose is complex. Too often we rely on ensuring that children write with correct punctuation and spelling, at the cost of seeing themselves as writers who use writing for a variety of purposes. We tend to rely too much on paper and pencil as the only tools to support writers. In this chapter, we show you how to use drama, drawing, freewriting, personal correspondence, and coding as tools to show your emergent bilingual students the possibilities writing can afford them.

Drama

Drama is a powerful multimodal technique for supporting all students' reading and writing, but especially that of emergent bilingual students in all grades. It enables students to bring life to a story or explore the details in a text—details the audience needs to fully understand the text. When you bring drama into your classroom, your students will use their bodies, use their bodies and facial expressions, and work with props to express themselves and interpret the text (Whitmore, 2015).

There is an intricate connection between reading and writing when thinking about drama. Drama enhances children's comprehension of texts, heightens their language development, helps them summarize text orally and in writing, and builds vocabulary and oral language (Cornett, 2011; Deasy, 2002). You can examine through drama the nuances in the author's choice of words. Drama engages students on multiple levels—intellectually, kinesthetically, and socially—making it ideal for all types of learners. And, of course, it allows children to use their entire linguistic repertoires. As the teacher, you can take on many roles: fellow actor, director, audience member, guide, and so forth. When you assume the role of a fellow actor, you will likely build the confidence of students who may be reluctant to perform with classmates. In particular, drama is a powerful tool for emergent bilinguals, as it provides them with another "language" in which to express themselves and think about complex texts.

While reading aloud, you may stop to ask your emergent bilingual students to act out how a character feels. This is a great opportunity to explore words and nuances in their meanings—*angry*, *mad*, and *furious*, for example. You should also provide translations of those words in the languages the children speak, write them on chart paper, and help children explore their meanings using language, movement, print, and their entire linguistic repertoires.

Also, encourage your emergent bilingual students to dramatize pieces of their own writing to help them notice, for example, whether it flows or contains sufficient detail. Dramatizing their own writing also gives them a deeper sense of audience, since, presumably, they would present to their peers who can provide immediate feedback about what is clear and what isn't. It also helps them check descriptions of characters' feelings, such as happiness, delight, fear, anger, and embarrassment.

Drama can help students rethink traditional texts in imaginative ways. For example, students might compose as a class a more critical and feminist take on a traditional fairy tale, such as "Sleeping Beauty" or "Rapunzel," using translanguaging and capitalizing on their entire linguistic repertoires.

Kindergarten students read and act out text during center time in a dual-language bilingual classroom.

Drawing

While drawing is the entry way into writing for young children, it often gets put aside once children leave the early childhood grades. Drawing is a powerful tool to support your emergent bilingual students' writing across all grade levels. In order to use drawing to its full potential, you can assist them in noticing drawings around them—for example, in fellow students' work and in books that they read. That way, they will become readers of illustrations and use ideas from others to enrich their own writing. Help the children notice the ways in which illustrators often draw on their cultural backgrounds to create their illustrations. Drawing can serve several purposes to support and enhance writing.

Drawing as a Way to Understand the Writing Process

In her book *In Pictures and in Words*, Katie Wood Ray (2010) asserts that through drawing, students can learn about the complex processes in which writers engage. Your emergent bilingual students may also add to these drawings or revise them, much like they do with their texts during the writing process.

Drawing to Generate Ideas for Writing

Your emergent bilingual students can draw before they write in order to gather and develop ideas. For example, you can ask them to draw an image they remember from a favorite moment with a parent or another relative. After drawing, students can talk about their image and then move on to drafting.

Into the Classroom

Drama as a Powerful Multimodal Technique

Ms. Parra teaches in a Spanish dual-language second-grade class. She has read aloud *¡A bailar!/Let's Dance!* by Judith Ortiz Cofer (2011) to her students and has discussed it with them. Now, she selects one section of the story in Spanish and tells the children they will dramatize it. She displays the section with a projector and tells the children, "Voy a leer en voz alta esta escena de la historia, *¡A bailar!/Let's Dance!* Mientras la leo, quiero que la dramaticen (que pretendan que son los personajes de esta escena)." [While I read, I would like you to dramatize the scene (that you pretend you are the characters in this scene).] She invites a small group to the front of the room, gives each child a role, and adds, "Entonces, tienen que escuchar con mucho cuidado a cada palabra que leo, así la pueden llevar a cabo con su cuerpo, la expresión de la cara, los movimientos de las manos, y así por el estilo." [I am going to read aloud this scene of the book, *¡A bailar!/Let's Dance!* While I read it, I want you to dramatize it. So, this means you need to listen attentively to each word I read, this way you can dramatize it with your body, facial gestures, hand movements, and so on.] Ms. Parra reads the scene, and the children dramatize it, while their classmates watch. When she notices children struggling with certain actions, she slows down. She asks

Marta to translate the word *ritmo* into English *rhythm*, so Jeremy can better understand the scene. While Ms. Parra claps, Marta moves to the beat. Ms. Parra talks to the children about how music has rhythm (pattern). They talk about how *rhythm*

is a cognate, because in Spanish the word is *ritmo*. On the chart paper, she writes the letters that are the same in the same color marker, and in another color marker, she writes the letters that are different. Later, they will examine in more detail the spelling of these two words. Ms. Parra continues reading the text. She writes words on the board—*preocupada, emocionada,* and *feliz*—and helps the children study subtleties in their meanings by asking them to dramatize them.

Ms. Parra asks the children to think about why it is important for authors to use details in their writing. Julia shares that details help her create a picture in her mind. She says, "Era como una foto." Ms. Parra reminds the children that they will be working on this as writers—on describing scenes so clearly that their readers will be able to create pictures in their minds.

Writing Techniques, Tools, and Possibilities

175

Ms. Parra continues asking the children to dramatize stories to help them as writers. The next day, she chooses emotions: *triste* [*sad*], *enojada* [*angry*], *feliz* [*happy*], *cansada* [*tired*], *agotada* [*exhausted*]. She begins with *enojada*. As a class, the children dramatize what it feels like to be angry, using their bodies. Then they describe how their bodies feel when they're angry. Ms. Parra takes notes. Next, she divides the class into small groups and gives each group a word to act out. When they are done, each group writes a description of how they dramatized the word and then shares their description and dramatization with the whole class.

Drawing to Add Details to Writing

Students may draw to spur ideas or provide details that they are unable to express through writing. They may create simple pencil-and-paper sketches, or more sophisticated works, using a variety of media (e.g., paints, pastels), or technology. Students can talk while they draw to explain actions, events, or the emotions of a certain event.

Drawing and Writing Fiction

Wessels and Herrera (2013) cite a variety of ways writing and drawing intersect when writing fiction. They describe how the process of visualization while drawing enables students to "create a mental image" prior to writing about it, which helps emergent bilingual students gather ideas and organize their thinking during the writing process. Furthermore, these researchers state that by drawing, students develop a plan for writing and add details to it.

As you work with students, help them notice how the visual images add and complement the story. You can, for example, help children notice how one of the techniques illustrators can use is to craft tone with color. An illustrator might, for example, use gray to show sadness and spring colors to show renewal. You can help children notice how color can support a reader to more fully understand the emotions of a character. It matters that you take the time to slow down and look closely at the illustrations as you help children describe them (Colomer, Kümmerling-Meibauer, & Silva-Díaz, 2010) using their entire linguistic repertoires.

Drawing and Writing Informational Texts

Adoniou (2013) found that drawing also aids students in writing informational text. She documented that students who drew as part of creating informational texts wrote longer pieces than students who did not. In addition, students scored higher on a rubric designed to measure quality of writing. It is important to remind children that scientists often use drawing as a tool to document their learning and express ideas effectively.

Recommended Reading

In Pictures and in Words: Teaching the Qualities of Good Writing Through Illustration Study by Katie Wood Ray (2010).

Freewriting

There are many reasons to engage children in a freewrite, but the most important one is to open up the floodgates for writing, and to facilitate thinking. In other words, to write without censoring oneself. Peter Elbow (1998) writes, "The goal of freewriting is in the process, not the product" (p. 13). The writer might change topics in the middle or find him- or herself with nothing to write about at all. When that happens, the writer should just write, "I have nothing to write" as many times as necessary and move on when something new comes to mind. For emergent bilinguals, freewriting provides an opportunity to write using their entire linguistic repertoires, without adhering strictly to one language or another.

Elbow (1998) adds that writers can at times feel anxious when faced with a blank piece of paper. They can also feel anxiety in the middle of writing a piece. Freewriting can serve as a warm-up and help the writer get started and/or keep going. New topics can emerge as a result of regular freewriting.

Freewriting can support the development of emergent bilingual students' critical-thinking abilities and voice because it helps them become comfortable with writing (Wang & Zeng, 2014). It can also provide room to explore difficult issues they might be facing (Lannin, 2014), as well as to imagine and discover new possibilities or ideas for writing (Janks, 2014). Follow this process each day:

Create a regular time for your emergent bilingual students to engage in freewriting. Make sure you model by writing with them and invite them to use their entire linguistic repertoires. Be sure to tell children how long they will write. Devote about three minutes initially to freewriting, and move to 10 minutes as your students become more disciplined.

Remind students what to do if they are stuck. They might, for example, write, "I am stuck" several times until they think of something more original to say. What is important is for them to know that they can write. They should not worry about quality and correctness for now.

When they've finished writing, invite two or three students to share their work in whatever language(s) they wrote it in, while the rest of the class listens. At the end, have the class discuss the process: How did they feel as they were writing? Were they concerned about making errors, switching topics, the silence in the room? What surprised them?

Double-Entry Journals

Double-entry journals are one of the "writing to learn" strategies outlined by the New York City Writing Project (NYCWP). Avidon (n/d) states that this writing experience allows the student to become actively engaged with the content by having a conversation with the author(s) or "thinking aloud" through writing. We add that by inviting students to capitalize on their entire linguistic repertoires, students can make connections between the content of a text and their own lived experiences. This informal writing tool can be used over time as students gather information and move to more formal writing (essay, project report, etc.).

Double-entry journals allow students to personally connect to a text using their language resources.

In a double-entry journal, students are asked to divide a paper in two columns. On the left-hand side, students write a quotation from the text they are reading with appropriate references (page number, author, year, etc.). This quotation can be in English or another language. In the right-hand column, students write their personal responses to the quote. Students can include agreements, disagreements, confusions, connections to lived experience, or questions for the author.

Personal Correspondence: Letters, Emails, Texts, Notes, Diaries, and Journals

Regardless of the language we speak, we communicate in writing on a regular basis, whether it's by writing letters or sending texts and emails. We also correspond with ourselves when we keep a diary or journal. Written correspondence is ideal for emergent bilingual students because the writer selects the language in which it is composed by keeping in mind the audience. What makes the process of writing a letter or an email special is that it is personal, even if it is formal. Your emergent bilingual students can write, for example:

- personal correspondence to parents, friends, visitors, teachers, or a tour guide from a field trip

- letters or emails to an author or illustrator

- a letter from the perspective of historical figure or a letter written to the historical figure

- thank-you cards

- a letter from the child to the parents about the child's work, for when the parents come to parent-teacher conferences

- letters or emails to a pen pal

- notes to classmates

- diary or journal entries

- letters to a character or letters from the character's point of view as a way to enter the world of story

There are many books written in the form of letters that serve as good models for students, including books for adults, such as *Between the World and Me* (2015) by Ta-Nehisi Coates, a letter he wrote to his son, which won the 2015 National Book Award Prize. At the end of this section, we offer a list of books for children that are written in letter form.

Letter writing offers students the opportunity to engage in authentic written dialogue. It helps emergent bilingual students discover that the purpose of writing is to communicate one's intentions, meanings, and wonderings and to develop or maintain a relationship. It helps students realize that audience is paramount. Letter writing is also a way for students to develop an awareness that their bilingual voices matter.

Letter writing can occur at many moments in your class's life. They can be written at the beginning or end of a unit. A classroom in which written dialogue is valued offers multitudes of genuine opportunities for children to engage in letter writing (letters, emails, postcards, texts, notes, etc.).

At its core, letter writing promotes dialogue between the writer and someone else. As such, the translanguaging possibilities for personal correspondence writing are many. Your emergent bilingual students can establish relationships with children from other countries, states, or schools. They can use translanguaging to construct meaning, communicate deeper meanings, and maintain a sense of audience. They can write letters to an expert on a subject. They can also write to people they know in the form of invitations, announcements, and thank-you cards. Because audience is central to letter writing, the possibilities for translanguaging are limitless.

Recommended Websites

Teaching Audience Through Interactive Writing readwritethink.org/classroom-resources/lesson-plans/teaching-audience-through-interactive-242.html

Mail Time! An Integrated Postcard and Geography Study readwritethink.org/classroom-resources/lesson-plans/mail-time-integrated-postcard-393.html

Note Writing in the Classroom readwritethink.org/classroom-resources/lesson-plans/note-writing-primary-classroom-285.html

Write Letters that Make Things Happen! readwritethink.org/classroom-resources/calendar-activities/write-letters-that-make-20572.html

Better Letters: Lesson Planning for Letter Writing educationworld.com/a_lesson/lesson281.shtml

Children's Books in the Form of Letters and Diaries

Amelia's Notebook by Marissa Moss (2006)

Dear Abuelo by Grecia Huesca Dominguez (2019)

Diary of a Spider by Doreen Cronin (2013)

Diary of a Worm by Doreen Cronin (2003)

El diario de Pedro por Pam Conrad (1993)

If You Come to Earth by Sophie Blackall (2020)

The Jolly Postman or Other People's Letters by Janet and Allan Ahlberg (2001)

Letters from Bear by Gauthier David (2020)

Letters from Space by Clayton Anderson (2020)

Los diarios de Cereza y Valentín por Joris Chamblain (2019)

Malú: Diario íntimo de una perra por Ignacio Martínez (2001)

Yo, Naomi León por Pam Muñoz Ryan (2005)

Coding Integrated With Writing

Technology in education means different things to different people. For example, some people may turn their thoughts to students using software to do their work or using apps that are created to help students practice academic skills. This use of technology can be referred to as technology literacy. However, the importance of students understanding *how these programs work and being authors of programs* through coding is critical. When students code, they use a programming language to write instructions or code that tells a computer what to do. Both coding and writing are composing and have a goal to communicate to an audience.

Computer science (CS) education, which includes coding, provides opportunities for students to not only understand how the programs that students use are created, but to enter into the conversation of how these programs affect them and what they want to "put out in the world" (Vogel, 2020). Emergent bilinguals are often left out of CS instruction and work with programs designed to strengthen their academic skills, yet by leveraging their social and linguistic resources, emergent bilinguals can be agents in learning (Vogel, Hoadley, Ascenzi-Moreno & Menken, 2019).

Student codes his Journey to School Project in Scratch, choosing Spanish to code in.

The integration of coding with writing provides an ideal instructional context to support students to learn CS skills, while also learning what it means to write. Designing CS units integrated with writing provides teachers with an opportunity to engage students in using their own resources to both code and take up writing skills in context.

A student creates a prototype for her coding project with objects and toys.

For instance, in one sixth-grade class, students were exploring how children around the world go to school (Ascenzi-Moreno, Güilamo, & Vogel, 2020). The teacher had students create and code a computer game about the way that they go to school. Before coding, students placed objects from home and school on hand-drawn maps to demonstrate how the journey to school would play out. Students then narrated their journeys to school to partners to explain how their program would work. This process of orally retelling an important event parallels what writers do when they compose a text. Through these conversations, students talked about their journeys to school and then linked them to how they would code them using a program called Scratch, a block-based program freely available (scratch.mit.edu). In this way, students learned that their narratives could take diverse forms—stories, text, and code. Like writing, coding also involves a process of composing that keeps in mind the needs of the audience. When kids move between named languages and code, they are also translanguaging.

CS integration with writing provides emergent bilinguals with opportunities to use their linguistic and social resources to talk about topics, writing, and code (Vogel, 2020). Scratch, which is available at this point in more than 50 languages, also supports students who may want to code in languages other than English. Coding, like writing, is a means of expression that shifts students' roles from consumers to producers, in which they express their ideas and share these with audiences. Knowing how to code and making links to literacies, such as writing, is a necessary skill for the 21st century.

For More on Coding

Participating in Literacies and Computer Science Video Showcase
www.youtube.com/watch?v=wotd9Meoos8

Please also visit www.pila-cs.org for resources on coding and literacy.

Action 12

Integrate Drama and Drawing in a Mini-Lesson

Mini-lessons are the bread and butter of writing instruction, but they must be carried out wisely. Too often, teachers talk about and demonstrate writing, and then send students off to write at their desks, alone, and then share with the class. While talking and demonstrating are important, this approach is not nearly as multimodal as it could be.

So, in Action 12, we ask you to breathe multimodality into your classroom as a way to support your emergent bilingual writers. By multimodality, in this case, we mean creating a lesson that integrates oral language, drama, and drawing. Often writing is connected solely to the traditional paper and pencil tools. Think about offering all students, including emergent bilinguals, multiple entry points to engage in and enhance writing.

To start, select a mini-lesson to adapt.

- You can, for example, use a mentor text that has translanguaging to examine the crafting technique of show, not tell (adding key details) through drama and drawing.

- Select a scene from the story that the children can dramatize and easily draw.

- Plan how you might explain to the children what a scene is.

- Plan how you might invite them to dramatize the scene in front of the class and how you will support

them by capitalizing on their entire linguistic repertoires to more fully construct meaning. For example, think about how you might group students.

- Prepare for reading the mentor text aloud to ensure you know it well.

- Plan how you will present the drama activity to the children.

- Prepare questions that will help the children see the importance of adding key details to a scene.

- On another day, plan how you will help the children see that authors paint pictures with their words.

- Plan how you might invite the children to draw the details in a scene from the mentor text. Children can, for example, work in small groups by selecting a scene and deciding who will draw what happened at the beginning, middle, and end. Invite them to share with the whole group.

Read your lesson plan over and ask yourself, what is at the heart of the lesson? Next, think about additional opportunities to engage students in multimodal experiences to support their writing development. For instance, how might you ask students to share their writing and help one another by dramatizing scenes in their stories? Plan how you can design these engagements so students can also work in small groups, capitalizing on their entire linguistic repertoires.

Reading as Writers: Using Mentor Texts

Emergent bilingual children can use mentor texts in powerful ways when our instruction is developmentally and linguistically appropriate. Good writers are typically voracious readers with a keen eye for noticing the details in texts. Furthermore, they intentionally integrate writing practices they learn from others into their own craft. In the words of Katie Wood Ray, writers "tune our writing voices to the writing voices we have known, much as our speaking voices are tuned to the voices we've listened to in the past" (1999, p. 72). Writers draw inspiration from other authors' craft.

Writing is a complex act that involves applying knowledge of register, conventions, and style.

Writing is a complex act that involves applying knowledge of register, conventions, and style. As Frank Smith (1983) noted, it is impossible to assemble everything one needs to know to be a good writer through prescriptive instruction: "We learn to write without knowing we are learning or what we learn. Everything points to the necessity of learning to write from what we read." Lancia (1997) found that his second-grade students engaged in a great deal of "literary borrowing" from the authors they were reading and used other writers as a "jumping-off point" for their own writing. Mentor texts also offer multilingual students the opportunity to extend their linguistic repertoires by using their home or new languages to try out and explore grammatical features, idiomatic expressions (turns of phrase), and other practices from the texts they read to write bilingual and monolingual texts (Espinosa, 2006; Laman & Van Sluys, 2008).

In essence, mentor texts are authentic models that emergent bilingual students can read and analyze as they try new and different kinds of writing. While at first your emergent bilingual students might emulate their favorite author, later you will see that they draw from a variety of other authors' techniques.

As a teacher, you have a responsibility to call your emergent bilingual students' attention to well-crafted writing, to guide them as they attempt new forms of writing, and then to encourage them to embrace those forms in their own writing (Griffith, 2010). As such, you must be the curator of mentor texts for your students. It's important to choose not only well-crafted texts that are pleasing to the ear, but also texts that mirror the linguistic and cultural diversity of your students and that contain a range of culturally relevant themes. If students are to learn from mentor texts, they must see themselves in those texts.

You might make mentor texts part of an author study unit. For example, elementary students might study the different ways Isabel Quintero, the author of *My Papi Has a Motorcycle* (2019), captures the passage of time by chronicling a motorcycle trip the main character takes with her father. The book also illustrates how authors use authentic dialogue by having characters speak, using their entire linguistic repertoires. By talking about what professional writers do, emergent bilingual students become aware of moves they might make to capture authentically the lives of bilingual characters in their own writing (Espinosa, 2006; Espinosa & Hudelson, 2007).

Over time you will find out that mentor texts can be used across the curriculum to help your students develop voices that are appropriate to discipline-specific genres. Just as mentor texts come in all genres, they also come in all languages. From these texts, your students might learn to use features from their named language, or they might learn to translanguage for a desired literary effect (see *CUNY NYSIEB Guide to Translanguaging in Latino Literature*, 2015; España & Herrera, 2020). Your students might also compare mentor texts across languages to notice the similarities and differences between literary expression in the two languages.

Depending on students' abilities in their home or new languages, mentor texts might be simple or complex. Even a short poem or nursery rhyme can be a mentor text, as long as it is an authentic example of good writing.

Recommended Picture Books for Teaching Writing

Go here for a list of picture books that can be used to model particular writing skills and literary elements: www.scholastic.com/teachers/article/mentor-texts-traits-writing.

Examining Authors' Crafting Techniques

All writers learn from other writers' craft. It is important that you take time to examine with your students the writing styles they enjoy and prefer. Encourage them to pay attention to translanguaging as a powerful writing technique.

Into the Classroom
Using Mentor Texts to Write Authentic Dialogue

The children in Ms. Ferrara's third-grade general education class have

been engaging in a personal narrative unit of study. They drafted seed stories after listening to Ms. Ferrara read aloud stories, mostly picture books, such as *Mango, Abuela, and Me* by Meg Medina (2017) and *Drawn Together* by Minh Lê (2018). Each child responds to the read-aloud with a story from his or her own life that in some way connects to one of the stories. Ms. Ferrara asks the children to share their stories orally with a partner. She has paired children strategically to ensure that those who want to tell their stories in their home language can do so. She reminds the children to "receive the piece," meaning partners need to be careful listeners. Partners take turns reading to each other and then write a response in their writer's notebooks.

Ms. Ferrara's class engages in this kind of shared writing and reading daily for about two weeks. Once the children have about 10 seed stories, they select one to draft further. From there, it is time for the class to study crafting techniques. Using a few of the stories she read aloud, Ms. Ferrara has decided to study with the class the following techniques: good beginnings, dialogue, show, not tell, and good endings.

Today the class is studying dialogue. While she projects the pages from *Mango, Abuela, and Me*, Ms. Ferrara asks the children how Meg Medina makes the characters talk in authentic ways. She asks them to describe what they notice. One student says, "The parrot speaks Spanish." Another child offers, "My grandfather speaks Chinese, and I don't understand everything he says," and yet another says, "I live with my grandmother, too, and she speaks Spanish."

The children notice that the characters are speaking in Spanish. So, Ms. Ferrara asks them to think about why that might be the case. Chavely replies, "Because that is how the family speaks." Ms. Ferrara replies, "Yes, we want to make sure we keep the dialogue authentic. Authors listen carefully to how people speak and sound. It would not make sense for the abuela to speak in English, even though the story you are writing might be all in English." The children and Ms. Ferrara examine the dialogue of the characters in another story, this time in English. She reminds them that when authors write dialogue in English, they use quotation marks.

Ms. Ferrara tells the children that when adding or revising dialogue in their drafts, they don't need to tackle the entire draft. She reminds them that all they have to do is try the technique on another page and label it as "crafting technique—dialogue." She asks them to return to their seats, reread their drafts, and find a section that contains or could use dialogue, modeling how to do so in her own story. She also reminds the children that they can continue to examine the collection of mentor texts for inspiration. As the children work on their drafts, Ms. Ferrara goes around the classroom, supporting them individually.

At the end of class, Ms. Ferrara asks a few children to share their revisions, using the projector to display them so the whole class can see how the writers applied the craft technique of dialogue writing.

Here's a way to get started. Gather excerpts from a text that contains translanguaging and that the students know well and might like to study more closely. We draw on Wood Ray's (1999) questions, modifying them to fit the needs of emergent bilinguals:

- What do you notice the author is doing with language?
- What words in this book sound interesting to me? Why?
- What do I notice about how characters speak in this story? Do all the characters speak the same language? Why is the author doing this? What can I call this crafting technique?
- Have I seen other authors use this craft before?
- How can I use this craft in my own writing?

As the teacher, it is your role to call attention to writers who may translanguage or use dialects that mirror your students'.

Lifting a Line

One way to teach emergent bilingual children to read like writers is to "lift a line." Lifting a line gives students the opportunity to savor language by exploring words, phrases, and sentences, particularly the language of authors who use translanguaging. In other words, it gives them experiences to read like writers by lifting lines or words from the page that are of particular interest to them.

We recommend you use a text that has translanguaging (poem, short story, chapter, etc.). It should be a text the children know well. Make sure everyone has access to the text. Ask them to spend time rereading it and find a word or a phrase that they want to share and lift from the page. Then ask the children to take turns lifting the word or line from the page, saying it out loud. The idea is to hear the words or phrases, to enjoy them, and to help children notice the sounds of words in other named languages.

Other Activities for Developing Writing Skills

Here are other writing activities that work especially well for emergent bilingual students.

Wall Talk

New York City Writing Project teacher consultant Diane Georgi (2007) describes "Wall Talk" as an "out-of-your-seat" interactive activity designed to engage an entire class in a silent conversation on a topic, question, or theme. When students participate in Wall Talk, they travel to different spots in the classroom to read and respond on chart paper to short passages of text. The "silence" of the activity forces students to use writing to express their opinions, reactions, or interpretations. At the same time, it encourages those who might not usually respond orally to share their thoughts in writing, along with everyone else (p. 1).

Visual Essay

This technique requires you to create a visual essay about a specific topic, such as immigration, community, the ocean, or the rainforest. You then display the visual essay on chart paper in the classroom or in a hallway, and ask students to write their responses to it, using their home languages and/or their new language. In a visual essay, you can ask them to respond to questions, such as:

- What do you see?
- What do you wonder?
- What surprises you?
- What is something you learned?

Text Graffiti

Text graffiti provides you with an opportunity to help your emergent bilingual students use writing to respond to a text as well as to their classmates' words. Text graffiti invites them to learn to distinguish their own words from those of an author or the words of other classmates. It helps your emergent bilingual students generate an expansive view of the different opinions that can exist about a text.

Prepare ahead of time by selecting excerpts from a book or a variety of poems. For example, if you are doing a unit on poetry, you can select poems in English and Spanish (8–10 poems). Give each student a copy of one of the poems. Ask students to read and respond to it, using their entire linguistic repertoires. Remind them that they can make a personal connection or a connection to another text. They can pose a question. They can draw an image or a symbol. When they are done, they move to the next seat. They read the next poem and respond in writing or with a visual. They can select a line in the poem that calls their attention. After students have responded to several poems, you can ask them to do a second round. This time they can reread the poem and also respond to their classmates' responses. Always remind them that it is okay to use translanguaging.

Recommended Reading

Wall Talk by Diane Georgi (2007), New York City Writing Project (NYCWP)

Text Graffiti: Previewing Challenging Topics by Jennifer Ochoa (n/d), Teaching Channel. Retrieved from www.teachingchannel.org/videos/preview-challenging-topics

The "Gist"

This technique can be used during your literacy block and also across all content areas, in particular, social studies and science. It requires students to write a short summary of a portion of a fiction or nonfiction text they have read. As such, students must read the text actively (Collins, 2012). The summary can be written in any form: bullets, phrases, complete sentences and/or drawings, on sticky notes or in notebooks, with students using their entire linguistic repertoires. As Fisher, Frey, and Hernández (2003, p. 43) state, "the ability to write a tight, concise, accurate summary of information is an essential entry point to other writing genres, especially analytical and technical writing."

A student writes the gist in Spanish on a sticky note when reading Social Studies content.

The primary purpose of this technique is to deepen students' comprehension. All too often emergent bilingual students read without taking stock of the crucial points in the text, and they do not leave evidence for teachers to understand what they are thinking (Harvey & Goudvis, 2017). When students summarize the text for the "gist" strategy, they learn from, reflect on, and remember what they have read. When they are invited to use their entire linguistic repertoires while using the strategy for academic texts, their understanding of content deepens (Espinosa & Herrera, 2016).

Be sure to model how to write a summary, thinking aloud as you go, before expecting students to do it themselves, in whatever language or languages they choose. If you teach younger children, encourage them to use text and pictures. Because the gist strategy is meant to capture each student's thoughts about the most crucial points in a text, translanguaging is a natural fit.

Book Review

Rather than asking children to write a summary, you can ask them to write a book review. When children write a book review, it helps them deepen their comprehension as they write to an authentic audience (future readers of the book). A book review also promotes the idea that reading is social, readers have opinions about the books they read, and that readers can share their opinions with the world.

After children read and examine some mentor texts of other children's book reviews, you can examine with them the key elements of a book review:

- Title and author
- The gist of what the book is about (without telling the whole story)
- Thoughts about the book's strengths and weaknesses from the reviewer's perspective. Ask them to provide specific examples, for example:
    - How did the writer of the review feel about the plot of the book and/or the characters?
    - Did the author make the reader feel like this world of story was believable? How did the author do this?
    - What does the reviewer like about the author's use of language?
    - Is there a section in the book that moved the child?
    - Would the reviewer recommend this book to other readers? Why?

Emergent bilingual students can review books written in one language and write a review in another, or even make a book review video.

Exit Slips

Exit slips are informal written assessments often used at the end of a lesson. They help the teacher get a snapshot of what the students have learned or what they are thinking about a particular aspect of curriculum. When using an exit slip, teachers often pose an open-ended question about a lesson and give the students a few minutes to respond. Students use writing in an exit slip to think about new concepts they've learned, to reflect on their learning, and to think critically and pose questions about it. As the teacher, your interest is in capturing what they know, what they understand, what seems confusing, and what they consider important.

Exit slips have many benefits. Teachers use what they learn from the exit slips to make changes in planning for instruction by addressing students' questions, interests, wonderings, needs, and so on. Through exit slips, you attend to students' voices. Exit slips offer your emergent bilingual students the opportunity to express their thinking, using their entire linguistic repertoires. This is not the time to assess their English.

Examples

Name:	Date:

Something important I learned today was:
Algo que aprendí hoy es:

Name:	Date:

My teacher could help me learn more about....
Mi maestro/a puede ayudarme a aprender más sobre....

Name:	Date:

A question I have about what I learned today is:
Una pregunta que tengo hoy es:

Recommended Reading

Exit Slips www.readwritethink.org/professional-development/strategy-guides/exit-slips-30760.html

Closing Thoughts

In this chapter, we introduced several techniques, tools, and possibilities—drama, drawing, coding, Wall Talk, among others—as options to enhance and engage emergent bilinguals' entire linguistic repertoires through writing. As a teacher, you are a master observer of children and crafter of curriculum. We ask you to combine your knowledge of children, writing, and pedagogy to craft multimodal lessons that support emergent bilingual students by engaging them fully in the writing process.

Suggestions for Professional Development

These activities are designed to help you reflect on how to further support emergent bilinguals' writing development.

1 Plan and carry out the lesson, utilizing one of the engagements described in this chapter. You can begin your planning by revisiting the lesson described in Action 12. Be intentional about how you invite the students to capitalize on their entire linguistic repertoires. You can plan with a partner or in a small group. Once you carry out the lesson with the students, think about how students participated in the lesson. Who participated, and how did they participate? Examine your emergent bilingual students' work, or if using drama, make a video of their dramatization. What do you notice about their participation and about their writing? How does it compare to their other work? What would you change about the lesson? How would you do things similarly or differently in the future?

2 Plan with a colleague how to integrate one of these engagements into a social studies, science, or math lesson. Think about what the content objective is, then think about how you want to engage the student through many modalities, including reading, writing, speaking, listening, but also drawing, acting, etc. Once you do this, you can match your content and goals for students' expression with one of the engagements we have described in this chapter. In your planning, identify the particular engagement, such as exit slips, drawing, writing a letter, using a mentor text for social studies or science. Make sure to demonstrate, if possible, how you use your entire linguistic repertoire to engage in the learning. While students are working, continue to use your powers of observation to understand how students engage in learning and how these engagements deepen their participation as writers in the content areas.

3 Engage in a freewrite alone or with another teacher. Pick a topic; it could be a unit of study that you are engaging your students in, or it could be an unrelated topic. Set a timer for about 5–7 minutes, and just write. Feel free to engage your entire linguistic repertoire. After finishing your freewrite, read your work out loud to one another and talk about which ideas stand out. Talk or think about how the ideas flowed. Which parts were easy and which were hard? What ideas opened up for you as you did your freewrite? What would happen if you did a freewrite using your entire linguistic repertoire daily, for 10 minutes for two weeks?

CHAPTER 10

Writing Assessment: Seeing the Emergent Bilingual Writer

"To take risks, to grow as learners, students must feel that they are known and that they know one another, including the teacher. Every school day, first to last, we need to demonstrate our curiosity about who our students are."

—TASHA TROPP LAMAN

The pioneers of the writing process advocated for assessing students by observing them as they write. Observing children and conferring with them regularly helps us develop a holistic understanding of children as writers (Graves, 1983). Graves and his colleagues knew that to truly improve writing, teachers needed to nurture the *writer*. To fully support writers, assessments must take into account a multiplicity of voices and diversity of language practices. Assessing students' writing monolingually does not reflect students' multilingual lives and practices. A translanguaging framework for writing assessment offers teachers both a strength-based vision of emergent bilinguals (Mahoney, 2017) and ways to account for students' use of resources across languages as they write. We start with the Prospect Center's Descriptive Review Process as a framework for seeing both the child and his or her work. This process is ideal for grounding writing assessment of emergent bilinguals because it starts from understanding the child as a learner and can be applied to understanding the child *as a writer*.

The Descriptive Review Process as a Starting Point for Writing Assessment

The Descriptive Review Process was developed by Patricia Carini and her colleagues at the Prospect Center in North Bennington, Vermont. It's based on a belief that when we compose a holistic portrait of a child as a learner and doer, we can fully attend to that child. The idea that teachers could generate knowledge about students was radical when the process was developed in the 1960s, and it still is in some places. At its core is the idea that as learners, we do not just receive the world—we engage with it.

The process helps teachers get to know their students deeply from multiple angles. It asks teachers to study the child in action in order to gain deeper understandings of him or her as a person through his or her work. This multilayered understanding of the child aids the teacher in meeting the student's needs (Espinosa, 2010).

> *The process asks teachers to study the child in action in order to gain deeper understandings of him or her as a person through his or her work.*

The Descriptive Review Process is collaborative. Teachers come together to think about and build knowledge about a particular child as a learner. This is a perfect starting point for assessing emergent bilinguals as writers, because the process gives teachers the opportunity to understand the whole child. It encourages teachers to study the children over time and across languages for their strengths, rather than focusing on what they cannot do.

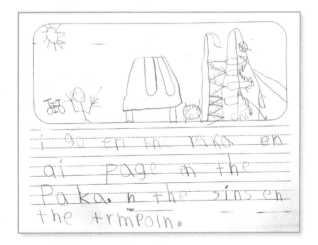

A young emergent bilingual student's work, perfect for Descriptive Review.

How the Descriptive Review Process Works

Carini and her colleagues developed many protocols to examine students, but we will highlight two of them: 1) the Descriptive Review of the Child and 2) the Descriptive Review of Children's Work (Strieb, with Carini, Kanevsky, & Wice, 2011). The difference between the two is that one focuses on the child as a learner, in this case as a writer, and the other focuses on the child's body of work across time.

The Descriptive Review of the Child

As teachers we have questions about our students: How can I support Dylan's productive partnerships with classmates? How can I help Leyla feel more connected to reading? How can I help Ana find topics to write about that matter to her and that help her develop her bilingual voice? The Descriptive Review of the Child (Strieb et al., 2011) begins with an open-ended question you have about a particular child and his or her learning. By exploring that question, you learn about the child in depth and enrich your knowledge base about teaching in general. As a foundational framework for writing assessment, the Descriptive Review process can be based on a question that truly matters to you, such as:

- How can I support Leo as a bilingual writer?
- What are Leo's strengths as a bilingual writer?
- How can I help Leo take risks as a writer as he taps into his entire linguistic repertoire?

The Descriptive Review can be done with other teachers during any professional development opportunity. You can ask new questions about different students, or you can ask a question about one student and ensure the question evolves over time. For example, a question at the beginning of the year could be, "How does this writer capitalize on his or her entire linguistic repertoire?". Then, by the end of the year, the question could be, "How has this child grown as a bilingual writer, and what do we need to do to support this writer as he or she prepares to move to the next year?".

Once you have selected a question, start gathering information about that child in five categories:

1. physical presence and gesture
2. disposition and temperament
3. relationship with children and adults
4. activities and interests
5. modes of thinking and learning

Observe the child through those individual lenses, asking yourself questions related to each, such as "How does the child relate to his friends?". A question like this one is tightly linked to developing a more a complete picture of who the child is as a learner, and in this way it influences how we teach writing. Teaching writing can never be separated from knowing who your students are.

When you have compiled information about the child according to those categories and examined a range of his or her work, present all the information you have gathered, along with the focus question, to a small group of colleagues. Make low-inference observations, or observations of the collection of work without judgment. At the end of the review, collaboratively make instructional decisions based on the child and his or her work as it relates to the focus question.

The Descriptive Review of Children's Work

The Descriptive Review of Children's Work (Strieb et al., 2011) parallels the Descriptive Review of the Child, as it begins with a question, but one that is based on the child's work (the work can be constructions, visual art, writings) created over the course of a unit, the entire year, or even more than one academic year. Once you've gathered and studied the work with your focus question in mind, present your findings to a small group of colleagues and talk about what you notice. This process allows you to identify what the child can do as a writer and how he or she does it. It is the perfect starting point to craft asset-based pedagogies for the student.

We need to avoid generalizations and abstractions and resist conventional explanations about emergent bilinguals.

When sharing information about the child and his or her work, we need to avoid generalizations and abstractions and resist conventional explanations about emergent bilinguals. It's also important to illustrate points with specific examples. Doing so enables us to fine-tune our observation capacities over time. We learn to describe in detail and take notes, which become important documentation to plan instruction. What we learn from this work should fold directly into our teaching.

Into the Classroom

Using Descriptive Review to Learn About a Student as a Writer

Ms. Castillo has been wondering how to best support Joaquín, an emergent bilingual child in her first-grade class whose writing intrigues her because he draws and uses only the letters in his name to write. Ms. Castillo is committed to examining Joaquín's writing from a perspective of strength. She wants to study what is in his writing, rather than what is not. Ms. Castillo selects samples of Joaquín's work, starting from the first month of school. It is February. (At her school, teachers keep a portfolio of each child's work throughout the school year and then pass it on to the next teacher.)

Ms. Castillo invites her grade-level colleagues and teacher assistants to meet with her to do a Descriptive Review of Joaquín's work. Before the meeting, she places samples of his work on a table, in chronological order. When the meeting starts, Ms. Castillo reminds everyone that comments must respect the child and his family. She also describes how the Descriptive Review process will be carried out:

1. Participants will spend time looking at the work, noticing first what stands out about it.
2. They will return to their seats and share their initial impressions.
3. Ms. Castillo, acting as chair of the session, will note what participants share. Immediately after, she will share recurring observations and themes with the group.
4. Everyone will decide on a piece to examine and describe closely.
5. Participants will share something they notice about the piece, starting with the very literal ("There is a yellow circle at the top-right corner that has lines coming out of it and appears to be a sun."), and moving to connections within the piece ("There are arches throughout the piece—rainbows, doorways"), to inferences and connections to other pieces in the collection ("I notice the people throughout the work are always smiling and have open arms."), and then offer recommendations to Ms. Castillo to support Joaquín as a bilingual writer ("Perhaps reading *Marta! Big & Small* by Jen Arena (2016) with Joaquín from a writer's perspective would help him compose a predictable story that features a bilingual character.").

Ms. Castillo will use her notes and the recommendations to think about how to nurture Joaquín's development as a bilingual writer. At the end of the session, Ms. Castillo thanks the participants for being respectful of the child and family and helpful to her teaching.

First and foremost, we want teachers to see emergent bilinguals as writers, and for that to happen, they need to see students beyond their finished work. We offer the following questions to assist you in constructing a more fleshed-out portrait of your emergent bilinguals as writers.

- How does the student listen and speak during writing mini-lessons? What language resources does the child use when speaking with adults and peers about writing?
- How does the student approach the writing task? Does he or she begin quickly, slowly, or somewhere in between?
- Before writing, when talking to peers about what to write about, what language resources does he or she use?
- What language resources does the student use while drafting? Is the child's internal dialogue in English, a language other than English, or both?
- When the student shares or responds to others' sharing, what language resources does he or she use?
- What languages are used and/or experiences conveyed in the student's writing?

By asking these questions, you will gain a clearer picture of how writing and language resources intersect for emergent bilinguals.

Writing Conferences From a Multilingual Perspective

As we shared in Chapter 8, writing conferences can take place while children are writing independently. The purpose of a writing conference is to understand what students are writing, to provide on-the-spot support, and to assess them and use this informal assessment in your instruction. Conferences provide an opportunity to learn about your students as they're engaged in writing and to provide feedback. Writing conferences should start with finding out what the child knows, which can be done by carrying out assessments described earlier in the chapter and arriving to the conference with a goal based on what you learn.

Action 13

Using Descriptive Review to Learn About a Student's Writing Over Time

Sarah Hudelson (1986), a bilingual educator, began researching emergent bilingual writers over 30 years ago. One takeaway from her research is that teachers must go beyond assessing emergent bilinguals' single pieces of writing and look at their writing over time.

In Action 13, we merge Hudelson's call with the Descriptive Review of Children's Work by looking at a bilingual child's writing over time (see Appendix A for a detailed description of this type of Descriptive Review). We invite you to select an emergent bilingual student in your class and collect multiple pieces of his or her writing over time. Place the pieces side by side on a flat surface and examine them. Pay attention to all aspects of the writing, not just conventions. If they contain drawings, think about what they convey. You can frame your examination of the work with a focus question or let the work speak for itself. Then assemble a group of colleagues and follow these steps:

1. Take turns stating what you see in the child's writing over time. Low-inference observations are best. For example, "The child wrote her name on the top, left-hand corner of the paper," or "There is a circle drawn with a blue crayon in the center of the paper," rather than, "This is great work."

2. Take turns with all the members of the group to continue to offer low-inference observations of the work.

3. Once everyone feels satisfied listing all of the things that they noticed about the student's work, the group will use these observations to start to construct a description of what the child can do.

4. Next, the chair of the group will offer a summary of noticings and impressions.

5. The group will then pick one piece of work to describe deeply. Teachers will take turns offering low-inference observations of just this piece of work.

6. Then the group will move to making connections between this piece of work and other pieces of work in the collection.

7. Lastly, the chair will open up the conversation to recommendations of what the presenting teacher can do to support the emergent bilingual child holistically.

In a writing conference, assessment and instruction are inseparable. Teachers are always informally assessing, and this assessment should immediately inform instruction. We discuss the following writing conferences in which you can both instruct and learn about your student through your interaction with them: 1) assessment; 2) supporting the writer's ideas and skills; 3) supporting the writer's good habits; 4) linking writing with mentor texts and/or audience; 5) supporting the writer as a multilingual person.

Assessment Conferences

We encourage you to find out about students as they are engaged in writing. What do you see? Do they talk about what they want to write about before writing? If so, what do they say, and in what language? What resources are they using? This is also the perfect time to involve students in the assessment process by asking them about how the writing is going. If you use the student's home language, the process will be easier and the instruction more effective. The questions that you ask should be open-ended and child-friendly—for example, "What are you working on?", "What is your next step?", or "What is something that you may need my help with?" These types of questions will lead you to information about what the child is working on and how you can support his or her practice.

Conferences for Supporting the Writer's Ideas and Skills

During writing workshops, teachers typically introduce a variety of ideas and skills to the class, such as adding details, adding and labeling text features, adding dialogue, and providing transitions. How do we support students as they work on those skills and ideas independently? Conferences are one way to understand what they learned, how they apply it to their writing, and how to support their development. For example, while working with a kindergarten student, you could start off by asking the child to talk about his or her work. Then you could refer back to the lesson in which you modeled how to add details to a drawing. You could then ask the student to try that idea or skill, all the while encouraging the student to use his or her entire linguistic repertoire.

Conferences for Supporting the Writer's Habits

Writing is hard for everyone, but it can be especially hard for young multilingual students. Orchestrating the physical demands of writing, as well as the mental demands of deciding what to write and how to write, is a challenge for all children. But when those children are writing in a language that they are simultaneously learning, it can be downright overwhelming. That's why they need to learn habits that will keep them on track as writers.

Like all conferences, your focus should emerge from what you know about the child, but with a particular focus on his or her writing habits. Does he take a long time to start? Is she always talking to other children at the table? Does he write one word and then wait for your help with spelling? Of course, there will be students who exhibit one or more of these habits. But for the conference, it is important to focus on just one to avoid overwhelming the child. Let's take Elvira, who recently came from Ecuador. She begins to write by drawing but needs help moving from pictures to words. One way that the teacher could support her is by talking to her in her home language prior to writing so that she can more fluidly generate ideas. If that is not a possibility, her teacher could show her some resources that she could use to help her write, such as picture dictionaries and illustrated sentence stems.

Conferences for Linking Writing to Mentor Texts

Good writing is nurtured by reading, and it is crafted by paying attention to audience. That's why it's important to always bring to conferences an appreciation of texts, authors, and audience. Texts should be diverse and represent the classroom community and communities in your town, state, and entire country. That way, students see themselves reflected in books, as well as others who may be different from them but share similar experiences. For emergent bilinguals, this also means sharing books that are multilingual and written for multilingual readers. For instance, you could share a book you've read aloud to the whole class, such as *Mango, Abuela, and Me* by Meg Medina (2017). Then, in a conference, point to the dialogue, which is in both English and Spanish, as an authentic example of talk among family members.

Conferences for Supporting the Writer as a Language Learner

All students are language learners, but emergent bilinguals are learning a second and perhaps even a third language. In a conference, you can demonstrate how to write bilingually or in one language. One way this could work is by first talking to students about what they want to write. Then you could support the writer by providing words or phrases that the writer will need. You could also do a quick review of language features, such as irregular verbs or prepositions, that the writer may need to work on. This type of support is not the goal of the conference but a means to aid the writer to express what he or she would like to. Regardless of the language in which the child is writing, all conferences should be based on what the child knows and lead to an appropriate next step for him or her.

Growing as Writers Through Self-Assessment

In their seminal book, *The Writing Workshop: Working Through the Hard Parts (and They're All Hard Parts)* (2001), Katie Wood Ray and Lester Laminack identify three types of questions that students could ask themselves to support their writing development and their identities as writers: questions of history, questions of action, and questions of process. Questions like these can be posed to the entire class during mini-lessons or conferences. Regardless of the context in which you ask the questions, make sure students understand them and give them the support they need to answer them. We offer examples of questions that keep Wood Ray and Laminack's original intention, but can be posed to emergent bilinguals, that are focused on how emergent bilinguals' language practices surface in their writing.

Questions of history are about how students see themselves and their writing over time. For younger students, this time period may be a week. For older students, it may be the entire year. Students ask themselves how they have grown as writers or developed through writing a particular piece.

- What do I notice as you look at my work? In what ways have I grown as a bilingual writer?

- What languages do my audiences speak, and how does my writing reflect attention to those audiences?
- How do I use language throughout my work?

Questions of action are related to things students do to support their development as a writer, such as noticing the writing in their favorite books.

- Who are some of my favorite bilingual authors whose work helps me as a bilingual writer?
- What have I learned about those authors?

Questions of process are about what students are doing during the writing workshop.

- What is something I have learned about myself as a writer? What helps me write? What does not help me write?
- Who is my audience? How does my writing speak to my audience?

Classroom-Based Assessment of Writing Pieces

The types of assessments you choose determine the information you get and your perspectives on students. While so far we have presented how you can assess their writing development over time and in conversation with them (through conferences and questions), we realize you may also want to assess single pieces of writing that result from, for example, a genre-specific unit.

Checklists and Rubrics

Checklists and rubrics are incredibly helpful tools for a variety of reasons. They give us very specific aspects of our students' process and product to look for. It's easy to find many checklists and rubrics online, but be sure to choose them carefully and for specific purposes—and never let them replace your own assessments of and reflections on your students and their work. We believe that the process of crafting classroom-based assessments and reflecting on results can be powerful. By creating your own checklists and rubrics, you align your writing curriculum, students' needs, and assessments. Although it may take time, we believe it will make you a better teacher of writing to emergent bilingual students.

It is critical to be intentional about the purpose of the classroom-based assessments you create and use—to gain information that will assist you as you support students' writing development.

If the checklist or rubric is written in a child-friendly manner, students can also use it to reflect on their development. If you introduce it at the beginning of a unit of study, students will have tools to think about their work, according to specific criteria.

If you're working with students on a specific genre, you'll need an assessment that focuses on that genre and both their process and product. We found a useful structure in Stead's *Is That a Fact?* (2001). Stead is careful to think about the features of nonfiction genres (headings, captions, instructions), as well as the language features of those genres (past tense, commands, quantity), that students need to learn so they can write in that genre. We believe that these features, combined with a space for translanguaging, lead to classroom-based writing assessments that are purposeful, intentional, specific, and geared to viewing emergent bilinguals from a strength-based perspective.

Find a blank form online at scholastic.com/RootedResources.

My Mom's Birthday
by Berta

It was my Mom's birthday. She was turning 38 years old. I woke early and ran to my parent's bedroom. "¡Feliz Cumpleaños!" I said to her while I gave her a big hug.

She said with a soft smile and her eyes filled with tears, "Es cierto, hoy es mi cumpleaños."

She walked into the kitchen and asked my Dad who was already making breakfast for the family, "Ramiro, no me vas a hacer una fiesta?"

He said in a serious voice, "no te voy a hacer una fiesta este año. No tenemos dinero."

With tears in her eyes, she said, "OK, Ramiro and [Berta] apúrense que van a llegar tarde a la escuela y necesito ir al trabajo."

While my mom went to work and we went to school, my dad said to my little brother Esteban, "apúrate, tenemos muchas cosas que hacer."

He had decided to stay home that day and prepare everything for a surprise party for my mom. They went to the store to by the food, rented tables and chairs, and when everything was set, my dad said to my little brother, "Esteban traime el teléfono, tengo que llamar a tus tios y tias para recordarles que deben estacionar los carros lejos de la casa, ...the ..." And the ...he boys ...veryone ...los ...npoline ...time to ...rning he ...ar."

Checklist for Language Practices Within a Personal Narrative

Features of Personal Narrative	How does the student do this?	How does the student use language/ translanguaging?
How does the writer use language to show what happened in the personal narrative?	The writer uses both dialogue between characters like,"¡Feliz Cumpleaños!" and explanations like, "he had decided to stay home that day."	The writer uses Spanish for the authentic dialogue between family members.
How does the writer use language that shows when the event happened?	The writer uses words and phrases like, "it was, while, early"	In the dialogue, the speaker uses words, phrases, and verb tenses to show time: apúrate, sospechará.
How does the writer use language to demonstrate who the characters are or how the person is related to him or her?	The writer uses words like, "my mom, my dad, my little brother Esteban, tios and tias."	The student uses both words in English and Spanish to refer to family members.

Into the Classroom

A Teacher Models Writing and Assessment

Mr. Vonn's second-grade class is engaged in a writing unit on personal narrative. Before the unit begins, he gathers information about teaching personal narratives and combines what he learns from the texts with what he knows about his students. By going through this study process, he is able to establish a clear purpose and goals for the unit that match his students' needs.

He starts the unit by modeling how to think about and write a personal narrative, highlighting the features of personal narratives and their purposes. While writing his piece for the class, Mr. Vonn incorporates translanguaging to demonstrate the importance of using his entire linguistic repertoire in authentic ways. Here is his piece:

The Chocolate Chip Escapade

One spring afternoon when I went to the kitchen, I saw my two boys, Matias and Tomas, in the pantry. When they saw me, I knew someone was up to something tricky because they started to run! They were stealing and eating chocolate chips from a bag in the pantry. When they started running, I yelled, "¡Niños, vengan aquí!" The bag with the chocolate chips split open, and all the chocolate chips fell to the floor. The next thing I knew, they stopped running, and they went down on all fours. They started eating the chocolate chips off the floor with their mouths instead of picking them up. They looked like little puppies, and we all started to laugh.

Next, Mr. Vonn highlights features of this personal narrative and explains why they are important. For example, he highlights when the event happened, who was involved, how the event unfolded, and what he and his sons said and in what languages. He then helps the children think about the language or languages they'll use to write their personal narratives.

As he plans how he is going to assess his students' writing, he creates a table to demonstrate how each feature of a personal narrative connects to language (see chart on next page). Highlighting the important parts of a personal narrative makes language teaching and use both explicit and intentional for both teachers and students.

Once Mr. Vonn connects the language that goes with each feature, he teaches both in tandem. By doing so, he supports emergent bilingual students in writing personal narratives and learning language in an integrated manner. It also helps him distinguish writing competencies and language features when assessing his students.

Features of Personal Narrative	Language Needed for That Feature
Telling what happened	Verbs in past tense
Telling when it happened	Language that identifies time: one day, long ago, last week, yesterday, when I was …
Telling who was there	Identify the relationship between the author and a person: my mom, my best friend, my cousins Julie and Miguel, the kids on the block …
Telling what happened in a sequence	Transition words: then, all of sudden, after that …
Using dialogue	I said, they scream, we whispered … (The statements are a perfect opportunity to use the students' entire linguistic repertoires, such as weaving in named languages from the communities they participate in.)

Instruction That Emerges From Observing and Knowing Children

Many educators believe assessment should be data-driven, but we believe it should always be student-driven. How does your knowledge of students help you think about writing instruction in general, but also about writing instruction for the whole class, as well as individuals?

Knowing your students deeply—knowing about their families, their interests, and their learning styles—helps you select materials and modalities for your literacy curriculum in general, and your writing program in particular. In addition, knowing about students' language resources helps you bring in multilingual texts and offer students opportunities to write multilingually.

When it comes to modalities, some students may need physical activity before writing more than others. For example, kindergarten students may need to retell a story by acting it out or using puppets before attempting to retell the story on paper. First graders may need to make pudding (and eat it) before sitting down and writing the recipe (a procedural text). Fourth graders may need to read picture books, watch videos, or visit a museum while working on pieces about the history of the community where they live. Regardless of grade, though, all students need opportunities to process in language that is authentic to them.

Knowing your students deeply—knowing about their families, their interests, their learning styles—helps you select materials and modalities for your literacy curriculum in general, and your writing program in particular.

It is also important to think about which materials can be presented in English, in students' home languages, or both. Knowing your students also helps you think about texts and genres with which students may already be familiar. Remember, while some students may seem to lack typical school knowledge, they all have experiences. So, while they may not know how to write a descriptive report, they do know about things they are close to in their lives. The assessments described in this chapter help you plan instruction for the whole class and individual emergent bilinguals.

Closing Thoughts

In this chapter, we framed writing assessment as a holistic endeavor that aims to nurture the writer. Writing assessment is uncharted territory because, unlike reading assessment, it is not usually prescribed by schools, which gives you a unique opportunity to craft writing assessments that support emergent bilinguals. The work of the writing teacher is to understand emergent bilinguals as writers, to envision possibilities for sustaining their linguistic repertoires, and to scaffold their learning. You can accomplish that by understanding the purposes of particular writing assessments, as well as by engaging in assessment practices that offer insight into the child as a writer and his or her writing over time.

Suggestions for Professional Development

The following professional development activities can help you grow in the area of writing assessment through engagement with others..

1 Using the checklist for personal narrative as an example, think about how you can recognize and support students' language practices with other rubrics you typically use.

2 Collect the work of one emergent bilingual child from draft to published piece on your own or with a colleague. Use the process of describing children's work in the Appendix to do a description of a child's work. What do you learn about this particular emergent writer? What is the writer able to do? How does the student bring his or her entire linguistic repertoire to writing? Are there opportunities for his or her interests to be pursued through writing? Do you set up opportunities for emergent bilingual children to write collaboratively? Does this writer have multimodal opportunities to create texts? What are two areas you would like for the writer to develop further? What types of support or scaffolding would this writer need? What tools are available in the classroom to support this writer? What else could you add?

3 Record (audio and video) a writing conference with an emergent bilingual student. When you play back the recording, think about what kind of conference you conducted. What information did you learn about your student? What kind of feedback did you give back to the student? Did these two things match—what you learned about the student and how you supported them? After viewing the playback, what would you have changed about the conference? Were there opportunities to allow the child to respond, using his or her entire linguistic repertoire?

Rooting Your Work in Students' Strengths

"Teaching is not a monologue. It is dialogue. And after hearing what kids have to say, I've got to do something."

—CORNELIUS MINOR

Throughout this book, we offer possibilities for emergent bilinguals to come to literacy instruction as whole people. By that, we mean that their identities and capabilities as multilingual people are not left at the classroom door. Instead, they are recognized and incorporated into literacy instruction as essential ingredients. At the heart of our message is recognizing that shifts in how we view emergent bilinguals and their resources *are the impetus* for instructional change.

Carefully consider theories you hold regarding how emergent bilingual children develop as readers and writers. Those theories inform your instruction in powerful ways. In this book, we hope you found a space to think about how to create opportunities that value children's multilingual resources and promote creativity, love, and enjoyment. We also hope your literacy instruction is equitable and transformative.

We teachers must truly understand emergent bilingual children and their diverse contexts and backgrounds. Children challenge us not only to think differently but also to do things differently. We need to follow their lead. We advocate that teachers are learners and need to think about what they know about children as learners. In particular, rather than criticizing or devaluing students' language resources, we need to view them as essential to their learning and helping to forge deep literacy experiences for all students in the class, ultimately deepening your learning as a literacy professional.

In the past, we learned techniques to assist emergent bilinguals with an isolated lesson or by teaching them a particular skill. Professional books usually contained advice relegated to text boxes and sidebars. We propose to infuse the literacy block with the language practices of your students—that is, normalizing the students' bilingual and multilingual repertoires as powerful tools to support literacy development. We have presented ways to bring forward, throughout the literacy block, opportunities for students to use those repertoires. This call for reframing literacy is the centerpiece of equity. Equity for emergent bilinguals and other children who are minoritized cannot be achieved through efforts at the margins (Muhammad, 2020).

Literacy and, correspondingly, literacy instruction are not neutral (Brooks, 2020). How literacy is taught privileges certain identities, histories, and language practices, while it silences others or renders them as inadequate. If we truly want all students to be literate and participate deeply in literacy instruction, instead of seeking students' conformity, we need to find spaces of innovation and creativity where they are deeply engaged in authentic literacy practices. As García and Kleifgen write, the education community must "move beyond defining the process of literacy linearly and its products as being monolingual and monomodal" (2019, p. 15).

The ideas in this book grew from years of working with emergent bilinguals, reading the work of researchers and practitioners, and rethinking how the bilingual/multilingual child needs to be positioned from a perspective of strength. We hope you build off our ideas and make them your own. We hope the belief that bilingualism is a resource, that the norm in literacy instruction guides you, and that you view students' multilingualism as a strength. Our job as educators is to capitalize on, nurture, and sustain students' multilingual and social resources in and through literacy and to ensure our instruction is rooted to strengths. Meaningful change in literacy instruction starts with recognition that emergent bilinguals come to our classroom whole, and with their own histories and resources. We leave you with a quote, to the right, from Yuyi Morales' *Soñadores/Dreamers* (2018), which speaks to the power and richness of emergent bilingual students' strengths.

Somos historias.
Somos dos lenguas.
Somos lucha.
Somos tenacidad.
Somos esperanza.
Somos soñadores,
soñadores del mundo.

- - - - - - - - - - - - - - - - -

We are stories.
We are two languages.
We are lucha.
We are resilience.
We are hope.
We are dreamers,
soñadores of the world.

APPENDIX A

The Descriptive Review of Children's Work

The Descriptive Review of Children's Work parallels the Descriptive Review of the Child described in Chapter 10. A collaborative inquiry, it is based on the study of a child's works (constructions, visual art, writings) and leads us to understand the child's interests, perspectives, and ways of making sense of the world. As philosopher educator John Dewey (1938) once wrote, "Every experience is a moving force.... It is then the business of the educator to see in what direction an experience is heading... (p. 38).

A central idea to the Descriptive Review of Children's Work is seeing each child as complex and recognizing his or her particular strengths and interests and how he or she makes sense of the world. The Descriptive Review of Children's Work challenges us to use language with precision. It reminds us that when we talk about emergent bilingual children, we need to avoid generalizations and abstractions and resist conventional explanations. As we practice description, we learn to describe with attention to detail and we take notes of our sessions, and this becomes important documentation over time. In addition, what we learn from this work folds directly into our teaching.

In a Descriptive Review of Children's Work, the purpose is not to fix the emergent bilingual child but to focus on understanding the child and how he or she makes sense of the world. We are not just assessing an end product. Instead, we are studying an emergent bilingual child in action and in motion. At the center of this type of descriptive review are the following questions:

1. What does it mean to tailor learning to the learner when we work with emergent bilingual children?
2. How do we go about examining and reworking our educational plans so that they better support the efforts of each emergent bilingual child?

How is a descriptive review of a child's work carried out?

For the descriptive review of a child's work, select an emergent bilingual child whom you have a question about. The session is usually set between a teacher and another teacher who is selected to be the chair. They meet to plan the review of the child's work and select work to share with the group.

The session usually begins with an introduction of all participants. Next, the session's chair introduces the process. The chair talks about issues of confidentiality and respect. The chair also reminds the participants to refrain from language that judges and labels and instead to use descriptive language. The chair also reminds the group that there should not be cross talking. This way the group ensures that everyone is listened to.

The chair asks the presenting teacher to provide some context. This means the teacher briefly describes the child and the collection or work or the piece. Next, the chair goes over the procedures for describing children's work. For example, the chair usually offers the group time to look at the collection of work and asks participants to jot down and subsequently share their general impressions of the work.

The group then selects one piece of the emergent bilingual child's work to describe.

The group members read aloud or independently review the piece. This process has several rounds of descriptions.

First Round of Descriptions: The chair asks the participants to point out elements of the work—in other words, to offer very literal descriptions (what is on the page). The chair pulls together the threads heard during the sharing. Pulling together threads from everyone's observations sustains the energy and helps everyone to regroup.

Second Round of Descriptions: Next, there is a second round of noticing and describing literally what is on the page. In this round, the group members may shift to noticing patterns, recurring images, and connections.

Third Round of Descriptions: The participants continue to refine earlier descriptions. They bring up new aspects in the work not previously noticed. Now there are layers in the descriptions that the group members have put forward. The chair continues to take a few minutes to pull together threads heard.

Final Round of Descriptions: This round focuses on the emergent bilingual child's presence in the work. Here the group members consider where there is evidence of the child's hand or voice, the standards the child holds for himself or herself, the child's attention to detail or not. The group also compares this close looking to the entire collection of work of the emergent bilingual child, if it is available.

In closing, the chair asks to group to consider whether they were respectful of the child and his/her family and community.

What can we learn from describing one piece, instead of a collection of pieces?

You can learn a lot about a child from describing closely one piece of his/her work if you don't have access to the entire collection of the child's work. This process of looking closely at one piece of work often sparks interesting questions and new angles for thinking when observing the child. Be careful not to dismiss or generalize work. Keep the language descriptive and tentative. You can say, for example, "From where I am seeing," or "from this angle…"

What can we learn from describing a collection of pieces, instead of just one piece?

A collection of work is about one child that has been gathered over time. It allows us to see changes in the emergent bilingual child's ways of making things. The more work described and the more years the collection spans, the fuller the picture, and the more we learn about the emergent bilingual child's style, interests, and ways of creating order.

Why describe children's work?

Describing work is a reminder that children—all children—*are* makers. It is in the making that a child's mind grows, along with the child's imagination, understanding, etc. By making something, the child makes a world, and it is in the making of works that the emergent bilingual child discovers. Describing work enlarges the describer's appreciation for the work and deepens recognition of the maker.

For more information on the Descriptive Review of Children's Work, see Strieb, L. with Carini, P., Kanevsky, R., & Wice, B. (2011). *Prospect's descriptive processes: the child, the art of teaching, and the classroom and school*, revised edition. The Prospect Archives and Center for Education and Research, North Bennington, VT: cdi.uvm.edu/sites/default/files/ProspectDescriptiveProcessesRevEd.pdf

APPENDIX B

Recollection: Your Own Story as a Reader and Writer

If reading and writing are two of the most valuable things we do, it's important to examine our own habits, patterns, and attitudes we have developed over the years. So here we ask you to consider answers to two overarching questions, using the supporting "Before, While, and After Attending School" questions that follow to help you generate memories:

1. How did you learn to read and write?
2. What does this mean for you as a teacher of reading and writing?

From there, compose an essay or narrative of you as a reader and writer. Doing this exercise will help you envision the literacy environment you can create for your students.

Before Attending School

Try to remember experiences you had with written words before you first went to school.

- Did someone read to you or tell you bedtime stories? What was it like? Did you have favorites? What were they?

- Were favorite anecdotes often told at family get-togethers?

- What kinds of books and magazines were in your house?

- Did you go to a nursery school?

- Did you watch any educational TV shows?

- Did anyone make an active, conscious effort to teach you to read?

- Do you remember engaging in writing? Do you remember observing others write? What kinds of writing?

- Think also of the languages in which these literacy events took place. What did you observe? What do you recall doing as a reader and/or writer?

While Attending School

- Once you went to school, recall the teachers who taught you to read and write. (Try to remember names, physical appearance, tone of voice, etc.) Try to remember how they taught you.

- Did they teach you in two languages?

- Did they read to you? At a certain grade level, did they stop reading to you?

- Did they ever talk about what they read?

- Was there a classroom library? What materials were available in it?

- What kinds of writing activities did you engage in at school? Did you write your own books?

- Do you remember seeing your teacher write for different purposes? If so, what kinds of writing did you observe him or her do?

- Did you observe others write at home? For what purposes?

- Did you write at home? If so, what kinds of writing did you do at home?

- Think about translanguaging (use of your entire linguistic repertoire)— your bilingualism or multilingualism. Did you enjoy reading and writing in school, or did you read and write just because it was required?

- Do you recall having to read aloud in front of the class from a book or your own writing?

- Think about your junior and senior high school experiences. Did your reading and writing habits change?

- Was there a period of time in which you suddenly began reading and writing a lot more? What did you read? Why the sudden change? Or did you read and write less and less?

- How did your school reading and writing compare to your home reading and writing? Did you receive reading and writing guidance from your parents, a teacher, or a librarian—someone who made a difference?

After Attending School

Now that you are older, think about your reading and writing habits in your languages.

- Do you and your friends talk about books, websites, blogs, podcasts, magazines, news, and so forth?
- What kinds of books do you have in your collection at home?
- If you have children, do you read to them?
- Are there books you've always wanted to read?
- Do you use the public library?
- Do you talk about your writing? In what language?
- Are there stories you want to write? Have you ever written a story, poem, or nonfiction piece?
- Think about your reading and writing in your languages. How do you sustain them? What do you do to improve as a biliterate writer? How does translanguaging exist in your adult life?

Now that you have gathered some answers to these questions, consider what this means for you as a teacher of reading and writing of emergent bilinguals. What larger connections can you make from this reflection that inform your practice? How does your own story help you envision the kind of literacy experiences and environment that you offer your students? You can write in letter form to a colleague or anyone else you want to, or in narrative or essay form. As you compose, feel free to draw upon your entire linguistic repertoire.

CHILDREN'S BOOKS CITED

Ada, A. F., & Campoy, F. I. (2015) *¡Pío Peep!: Traditional Spanish Nursery Rhymes*. New York: Scholastic.

Ada, A. F., & Campoy, F. I. (2016). *Yes! We Are Latinos: Poems and Prose About the Latino Experience*. Watertown, MA: Charlesbridge.

Ada, A. F. (2012). *Me llamo María Isabel*. New York: Atheneum Books.

Ahlberg, A., & Ahlberg, J. (2001). *The Jolly Postman or Other People's Letters*. New York: LB Kids.

Alexie, S. (2016). *Thunder Boy Jr.* New York: Little, Brown Books for Young Readers.

Anderson, C. (2020). *Letters from Space*. Ann Arbor, MI: Sleeping Bear Press.

Anónimo. (2003). *Yo tenía diez perritos*. Málaga, Spain: Ediciones Ekaré.

Arena, J. (2017). *Marta! Big & Small*. New York: Scholastic.

Arena, J. (2019). *Salsa Lullaby*. New York: Scholastic.

Argueta, J. (2016). *Guacamole: Un poema para cocinar/A Cooking Poem*. Clive, IA: Turtleback Books.

Blackall, S. (2020). *If You Come to Earth*. San Francisco, CA: Chronicle Books.

Camper, C. (2016). *Lowriders to the Center of the Earth*. San Francisco, CA: Chronicle Books.

Chamblain, J. (2019). *Los diarios de Cereza y Valentín*. Madrid, Spain: Alfaguara.

Choi, Y. (2001). *The Name Jar*. New York: Dragonfly Books.

Cisneros, S. (1984, 2009). *The House on Mango Street*. New York: Vintage Publishers.

Cofer, J. O. (2011). *¡A bailar!/Let's Dance!* Houston, TX: Piñata Books.

Cronin, D. (2003). *Diary of a Worm*. New York: HarperCollins.

Cronin, D. (2013). *Diary of a Spider*. New York: HarperCollins.

David, G. (2020). *Letters from Bear*. Grand Rapids, MI: Eerdmans Books for Young Readers.

Daywalt, D. (2013). *The Day the Crayons Quit*. New York: Philomel Books.

de la Peña, M. (2015). *Last Stop on Market Street*. New York: G. P. Putnam's Sons Books for Young Readers.

Dominguez, A. (2013). *Maria Had a Little Llama/ María tenía una llamita*. New York: Henry Holt & Co.

Dominguez, A. (2018). *How Are You?/¿Cómo estás?* New York: Scholastic.

Dorros, A. (1997). *Abuela*. New York: Puffin Books.

Flores, B. *Mud Tortillas*. New York: Lee & Low Books.

Franklin, A. (2019). *Not Quite Snow White*. New York: HarperCollins.

Henkes, K. (1991). *Chrysanthemum*. New York: Mulberry Books.

Jiménez, F. (2000) *La Mariposa*. New York: HMH Books for Young Readers.

Jules, J. (2015). *Sofia Martinez* (series). Minneapolis, MN: Picture Window Books.

Khalil, A. (2020). *The Arabic Quilt: An Immigrant Story*. Thomaston, ME: Tilbury House Publishers.

Khan, H. (2018). *Golden Domes and Silver Lanterns: A Muslim Book of Colors*. New York: Scholastic.

Lê, M. (2018). *Drawn Together*. New York: Little, Brown Books for Young Readers.

Lindstrom, C. (2020). *We Are Water Protectors*. New York: Roaring Brook Press.

López, R. (2018). *We've Got the Whole World in Our Hands*. New York: Scholastic.

Marsico, K. (2017). *Gorillas (A True Book: The Most Endangered)*. New York: Scholastic.

Martínez, I. (2001). *Malú: diario íntimo de una perra*. Montevideo: UY: Viejo Vasa.

Martinez-Neal, J. (2018). *Alma and How She Got Her Name*. New York: Candlewick Press.

Meddour, W. (2019). *Lubna and Pebble*. New York: Scholastic.

Medina, J. (1999). *My Name is Jorge: On Both Sides of the River*. New York: WordSong.

Medina, M. (2015). *Mango, Abuela, and Me*. Somerville, MA: Candlewick.

Medina, M. (2018). *Merci Suárez Changes Gears*. Somerville, MA : Candlewick.

Mora, P. (2019). *My Singing Nana*. Washington, DC: Magination Press.

Mora, P. (2005). *Doña Flor: A Tall Tale About a Giant Woman with a Great Big Heart*. New York: Knopf Books for Young Readers.

Mora, P. (2008). *Abuelos*. Toronto, ON: Groundwood Books.

Mora, P. (1994, 2011). *The Desert Is My Mother/ El desierto es mi madre*. Houston, TX: Arte Público Press Piñata Books.

Mora, P. (2003). *The Rainbow Tulip*. New York: Puffin Books.

Mora, P. (2000). *Tómas and the Library Lady*. New York: Dragonfly Books.

Morales, Y. (2015). *Viva Frida*. New York: Scholastic.

Morales, Y. (2018). *Dreamers*. New York: Penguin Random House.

Moss, M. (2006). *Amelia's Notebook*. New York: Simon & Schuster.

Muñoz Ryan, P. (2004). *Yo, Naomi León*. New York: Scholastic.

Nyong'o, L. (2019). *Sulwe*. New York: Simon & Schuster Books for Young Readers.

Orozco, J-L. (2020). *Sing With Me/Canta conmigo: Six Classic Songs in English and Spanish*. New York: Scholastic.

Perkins, M. (2019). *Between Us and Abuela: A Family Story from the Border*. New York: Farrar, Straus and Giroux.

Quintero, I. (2019). *My Papi Has a Motorcycle/Mi papi tiene una moto*. New York: Kokila.

Recorvits, H. (2014). *My Name Is Yoon*. New York: Square Fish.

Salazar, A. (2020). *Land of the Cranes*. New York: Scholastic.

Sorell, T. (2020). *We Are Grateful: Otsaliheliga*. New York: Scholastic.

Tonatiuh, D. (2010). *Dear Primo: A Letter to My Cousin*. New York: Scholastic.

Thompkins-Bigelow, J. (2020). *Your Name Is a Song*. Seattle WA: The Innovation Press.

Woodson, J. (2018). *The Day You Begin*. New York: Nancy Paulsen Books.

Woodson, J. (2001). *The Other Side*. New York: G. P. Putnam's Sons Books for Young Readers.

REFERENCES

Adoniou, M. (2013). Drawing to support writing development in English language learners. *Language and Education, 27*(3), 261–277.

Afflerbach, P. (2016). Reading assessment: Looking ahead. *The Reading Teacher, 69*(4), 413–419.

Allyn, P., & Morrell, E. (2016). *Every child a super reader: 7 strengths to open a world of possible*. New York: Scholastic.

Ascenzi-Moreno, L. (2016). An exploration of elementary teachers' views of informal reading inventories in dual language bilingual programs. *Literacy Research and Instruction, 55*(4), 285–308.

Ascenzi-Moreno, L. (2017). From deficit to diversity: How teachers of recently arrived emergent bilinguals negotiate ideological and pedagogical change. *Schools: Studies in Education, 15*(2), 276–302.

Ascenzi-Moreno, L. (2018). Translanguaging and responsive assessment adaptations: Emergent bilingual readers through the lens of possibility. *Language Arts, 95*(6), 355–369.

Ascenzi-Moreno, L., & Espinosa, C. (2018). "Opening up spaces for their whole selves": A case study group's exploration of translanguaging practices in writing. *New York State TESOL Journal, 5*(1), 10–29.

Ascenzi-Moreno, L., & Quiñones, R. (2020). Bringing bilingualism to the center of guided reading instruction. *The Reading Teacher, 74*(2), 137–146.

Ascenzi-Moreno, L., Güilamo, A., & Vogel, S. (2020). Integrating coding and language arts: A view into sixth graders' multimodal and multilingual learning. *Voices from the Middle, 27*(4), 47–52.

Avalos, M., Plasencia, A., Chavez, C., & Rascón, J. (2007). Modified guided reading: Gateway to English as a second language and literacy learning. *The Reading Teacher, 61*(4), 318–329.

Avidon, E. (n/d). Double-entry response. New York City Writing Project (NYCWP) and Elementary Teachers Network (ETN). Unpublished manuscript.

Batalova, J., & McHugh, M. (2010). Number and growth of students in U.S. schools in need of English instruction, 2009. Washington, DC: Migration Policy Institute.

Bauer, E. B., Colomer, S. E., & Wiemelt, J. (2018). Biliteracy of African American and Latinx kindergarten students in a dual-language program: Understanding students' translanguaging practices across informal assessments. *Urban Education, 55*(3), 331–361.

Beers, K., & Probst, R. (2017). *Disrupting thinking: Why how we read matters.* New York: Scholastic.

Berthoff, A. E. (1981). *The making of meaning.* Portsmouth, NH: Heinemann.

Briceño, A., & Klein, A. F. (2018) Running records and first grade English learners: An analysis of language-related errors. *Reading Psychology, 39*(4), 335–361. doi:10.1080/02702711.2018.1432514

Briceño, A., & Klein, A. F. (2019). A second lens on formative reading assessment with multilingual students. *The Reading Teacher, 72*(5), 611–621.

Brooks, M. D. (2020). *Transforming literacy education for long-term English learners: Recognizing the brilliance in the undervalued.* New York: Routledge.

Burkins, J., & Yaris, K. (2016). *Who's doing the work? How to say less so readers can do more.* Portsmouth, NH: Stenhouse Publishers.

Calkins, L. (1983). *Lessons from a child.* Portsmouth, NH: Heinemann.

Canagarajah, S. (2011). Codemeshing in academic writing: Identifying teachable strategies of translanguaging. *The Modern Language Journal, 96*, 401–417.

Cappellini, M. (2005). *Balancing reading and language learning: A resource for teaching English language learners, K–5.* Portsmouth, NH: Stenhouse Publishers.

Celic, C. (2009). *English language learners, day by day, K–6: A complete guide to literacy, content-area, and language instruction.* Portsmouth, NH: Heinemann.

Cioè-Peña, M. (2020). Raciolinguistics and the education of emergent bilinguals labeled as disabled. *The Urban Review.*

Clay, M. M. (1975). *What did I write? Beginning writing behavior.* Portsmouth, NH: Heinemann.

Clay, M. M. (1993). *An observation survey of early literacy achievement.* Portsmouth, NH: Heinemann.

Clay, M. M. (2000). *Running records for classroom teachers, 2nd ed.* Portsmouth, NH: Heinemann.

Coates, T. (2015). *Between the world and me.* New York: Spiegel & Grau.

Collins, J. (2012). "Summarize to get the gist." *Educational Leadership, 69.*

Colomer, T., Kümmerling-Meibauer, B., & Silva-Diaz, C. (Eds.) (2010). *New directions in picturebook research.* New York: Routledge.

Cornett, C. E. (2011). *Creating meaning through literature and the arts. 4th edition.* Boston, MA: Pearson.

Deasy, R. J. (2002). Critical links: Learning in the arts and student academic and social development, Washington, DC: Arts Education Partnership.

de los Ríos, C. V., & Seltzer, K. (2017). Translanguaging, coloniality, and English classrooms: An exploration of two bicoastal urban classrooms. *Research in the Teaching of English*; Urbana, *52*(1), 55–76.

Dorr, R. E. (2006). Something old is new again: Revisiting language experience. *The Reading Teacher, 60*(2), pp. 138–146.

D'warte, J. (2014). Exploring linguistic repertoires: Multiple language use and multimodal activity in five classrooms. *Australian Journal of Language and Literacy, 37*(1), 21–30.

Dyson, A. H. (2015). The search for inclusion: Deficit discourse and the erasure of childhoods. *Language Arts, 92*(3), 199–207.

Ebe, A. E. (2010). Culturally relevant texts and reading assessment for English language learners. *Reading Horizons, 50*(3).

Edelsky, C. (2003) Theory, politics, hope, and action. *The Quarterly, 25*(3), 10–19.

Edelsky, C., & Jilbert, K. (1985). Bilingual children and writing: Lessons for all of us. *The Volta Review, 87*(5), 57–72.

Elbow, P. (1998). *Writing with power: Techniques for mastering the writing process.* New York: Oxford University Press.

Emig, J. (1971). *The composing processes of twelfth graders.* National Council of Teachers of English.

Escamilla, K., Hopewell, S., Butvilofsky, S., Sparrow, W., Soltero-González, L., Ruiz-Figueroa, O., & Escamilla, M. (2014). *Biliteracy from the start: Literacy squared in action.* Philadelphia, PA: Caslon Publishing.

España, C., & Herrera, L. Y. (2020). *En comunidad: Lessons for centering the voices and experiences of bilingual Latinx students.* Portsmouth, NH: Heinemann.

Espinosa, C. (2006). Finding memorable moments: Images and identities in autobiographical writing. *Language Arts, 84*(2), 136–144.

Espinosa, C. (2010). Memory: Making and remaking ourselves as teachers. In M. Himley, and P. Carini, with C. Christine, C. Espinosa, J. Fournier. *Jenny's story: Taking the Long View of the Child: Prospect's philosophy in action.* New York: Teachers College Press.

Espinosa, C., Ascenzi-Moreno, L., & Vogel, S. (2016). Building on strengths: Translanguaging and writing. In O. García (Ed.) *Multilingual Students, Translanguaging and CUNY-NYSIEB.* New York: Routledge.

Espinosa, C., Ascenzi-Moreno, L., & Vogel, S. (2016). A translanguaging pedagogy for writing: A CUNY NYSIEB Guide for Educators. New York, CUNY NYSIEB. nysieb.ws.gc.cuny.edu/files/2016/04/TLG-Pedagogy-Writing-04-15-16.pdf.

Espinosa, C., Ascenzi-Moreno, L., & Vogel, S. (2020). Building on strengths: Translanguaging and writing. (In City University of New York state initiative on emergent bilinguals). *Translanguaging and transformative teaching for emergent bilingual students.* New York: Routledge.

Espinosa, C., & Herrera, L. Y., with Gaudreau, C. M. (2016). Reclaiming bilingualism: Translanguaging in a science class. In O. García and T. Kleyn (Eds). *Translanguaging with Multilingual Students: Learning from Classroom Moments.* New York: Taylor and Francis/Routledge.

Espinosa, C., & Hudelson, S. (2007). *Maestros y estudiantes como aprendices de nuevos discursos académicos. Teachers and students as apprentices of new academic discourses.* Revista Mexicana de Investigación Educativa (RMIE), *12*(34), 867–894.

Espinosa, C., & Lehner-Quam, A. (2019). Sustaining bilingualism: Multimodal arts experiences for young readers and writers. *Language Arts, 96*(4), 265–268.

Faltis, C., & Hudelson, S. (1994). Learning English as an additional language in K–12 schools. *TESOL Quarterly, 28*, 3, 457–488.

Fisher, D., Frey, N., & Hernandez, T. (2003). What's the gist? Summary writing for struggling adolescent writers. *Voices from the Middle, 1*(2), 43-49.

Fletcher, R., Portalupi, J. (2001). *Writing workshop: The essential guide.* Portsmouth, NH: Heinemann.

Fletcher, R. (2017). *Joy write: Cultivating high-impact, low-stakes writing.* Portsmouth, NH: Heinemann.

Fountas, I., & Pinnell, G. S. (2012). Guided reading: The romance and the reality. *The Reading Teacher, 66*(4), 268–284. doi: 10.1002/TRTR.01123

Fountas, I. & Pinnell, G. S. (2016). *Guided reading: Responsive teaching across the grades.* (2nd edition). Portsmouth, NH: Heinemann.

Freeman, Y., & Freeman, D. (2009). *La enseñanza de la lectura y escritura en español y en inglés.* Portsmouth, NH: Heinemann.

Fu, D. (2009). *Writing between languages: How English language learners make the transition to fluency*. Portsmouth, NH: Heinemann.

Fu, D., Hadjioannou, X., & Zhou, X. (2019). *Translanguaging for emergent bilinguals: Inclusive teaching in the linguistically diverse classroom*. New York: Teachers College Press.

García, O. (2009). *Bilingual education in the 21st century: A global perspective*. Malden, MA and Oxford: Basil/Blackwell.

García, O. (2020). Translanguaging and Latinx bilingual readers. *The Reading Teacher, 73*(5), 557–562. doi:10.1002/trtr.1883

García, O., Kleifgen, J. A., & Falchi, L. (2008). From English language learners to emergent bilinguals: A research Initiative of the Campaign for Educational Equity. *Equity Matters: Research Review No. 1*. New York: Teachers College, Columbia University.

García, O., & Kleifgen, J. A. (2019). Translanguaging and literacies. *Reading Research Quarterly, 55*(4),

García, O., & Kleyn, T. (Eds.). (2016). *Translanguaging with multilingual students: Learning from classroom moments*. New York: Routledge.

García, O., & Wei, L. (2014). *Translanguaging: Language, bilingualism and education*. New York: Palgrave Macmillan.

García, O., & Sánchez, M. T. (2018). Transformando la educación de bilingües emergentes en el estado de Nueva York. *Language, Education, and Multilingualism, 1*, 138–156.

Genishi, C., & Haas Dyson, A. (2009). *Children, language and literacy: Diverse learners in diverse times*. New York: Teachers College Press.

Georgi, D. (2007). Wall Talk Strategy. New York City Writing Project (NYCWP). Unpublished document. New York: Lehman College.

González, N., Moll, L., & Amanti, C. (2005). *Funds of Knowledge: Theorizing practices in households, communities, and classrooms*. New York: Routledge.

Goodman, K. (1967). Reading: A psycholinguistic guessing game. *Journal of the Reading Specialist, 6*(4), 126–135. https://doi.org/10.1080/19388076709556976

Goodman, K. (1996). *On reading: A common sense look at the nature of language and the science of reading*. Portsmouth, NH: Heinemann.

Goodman, K., & Goodman, Y. (2014). *Making sense of learners making sense of written language: The selected works of Kenneth S. Goodman and Yetta M. Goodman*. New York: Routledge.

Goodman, K., & Goodman, Y. (1991). The dialects of English and dialect differences and school programs. In K. Goodman, L. Bird, & Y. Goodman (Eds.) *The whole language catalog* (pp. 83, 85). New York: Glencoe/McGraw-Hill School Publishing.

Goodman, K., & Goodman, Y. (1991). Our ten best ideas for reading teachers. Fry, E., (ed.), *10 best ideas for reading teachers*. Addison-Wesley, 1991, 60–64.

Goodman, Y., Martens, P., & Flurkey, A. (2016). Revaluing readers: Learning from Zachary. *Language Arts, 93*(3), 213–225.

Goodman, Y., & Owocki, G. (2002). *Kidwatching: Documenting children's literacy development*. Portsmouth, NH: Heinemann.

Goodman, Y., Watson, D., & Burke, C. (1987). *Reading miscue inventory: Alternative procedures*. Katonah, NY: Richard Owen.

Gort, M. (2012). Code-switching patterns in the writing-related talk of young emergent bilinguals. *Journal of Literacy Research, 44*(1), 45–75.

Graves, D. (1983). *Writing teachers and children at work*. Portsmouth, NH: Heinemann.

Graves, D. (1994). *A fresh look at writing*. Portsmouth, NH: Heinemann.

Griffith, R. R. (2010). Students learn to read like writers: A framework for teachers of writing. *Reading Horizons, 50*, 49–66.

Harvey, S., & Goudvis, A. (2017). *Strategies that work: Teaching comprehension for understanding, engagement, and building knowledge, grades K–8*. Portsmouth, NH: Stenhouse.

Hawkins, L. (2016). The power of purposeful talk in the primary-grade writing conference. *Language Arts, 94*(1), 8–21.

Heard, G. (1999). *Awakening the heart: Exploring poetry in elementary and middle school*. Portsmouth, NH: Heinemann.

Heard, G. (2016). *Heart maps: Helping students create and craft authentic writing*. Portsmouth, NH: Heinemann.

Henderson, J., Warren, K., Whitmore, K., Seely Flint, A. S., Tropp Laman, T., & Jaggers, W. (2020). Take a close look: Inventorying your classroom library for diverse books. *The Reading Teacher*.

Himley, M., & Carini, P. (2000). *From another angle: Children's strengths and school standards*. New York: Teachers College Press.

Hornberger, N. H., & Link, H. (2012). Translanguaging in today's classrooms: A biliteracy lens. *Theory Into Practice, 51*(4), 239–247.

Horner, B., Lu, M. Z., Jones, R. J., & Trimbur, J. (2011). *College English, 73*(3), 303–321.

Hudelson, S. (1981). An introductory examination of children's invented spelling in Spanish, *NABE Journal, 6*:2-3, 53-67, DOI: 10.1080/08855072.1981.10668424

Hudelson, S. (1986). Children's writing in ESL: What we've learned, what we're learning. In P. Rigg and D. S. Enright (Eds.), *Children and ESL: Integrating perspectives*. Washington, DC: Teachers of English to Speakers of Other Languages.

Hudelson, S. (1989). *Write on: Children writing in ESL*. Englewood Cliffs, NJ: Prentice Hall.

Hudelson, S. (2005). Adding on English writing in a bilingual program: Revisiting and reconceptualizing the data. In P. Matsuda and T. Silva (Eds.), *Second language writing: perspectives on the process of knowledge construction*. Mahwah, NJ: Lawrence Erlbaum Publishers.

Hudelson, S. & Serna, I. (1994). Beginning literacy in English in a whole language bilingual program. In A. Flurkey & R. Meyer (Eds)., *Under the whole language umbrella: Many cultures, many voices.* (pp. 278–294). National Council of Teachers of English.

Hudelson, S. J. (2000). Developing a framework for writing in dual language settings. In J. V. Tinajero and R. A. DeVillar (Eds.). *The Power of Two Languages*. New York: McGraw-Hill.

Janks, H. (2014). *Doing critical literacy: Texts and activities for students and teachers*. New York: Routledge.

Johnson, L. P. (2018). Alternative writing worlds: The possibilities of personal writing for adolescent writers. *Journal of Adolescent & Adult Literacy, 62*(3), 311–318.

Kabuto, B. (2017). A socio-psycholinguistic perspective on biliteracy: The use of miscue analysis as a culturally relevant assessment tool. *Reading Horizons, 56*(1), 25–44.

Kabuto, B. (2018). Becoming a bilingual reader as linguistic and identity enactments. *Talking Points, 29*(2), 11–18.

Kibler, A. (2010). Writing through two languages: First language expertise in a language minority classroom. *Journal of Second Language Writing, 19*, 121–142.

Laman, T. T. (2013). *From ideas to words: Writing strategies for English language learners*. Portsmouth, NH: Heinemann.

Laman, T. T., & Van Sluys, K. (2008). Being and becoming: Multilingual writers' practices. *Language Arts, 85*(4), 265–274.

Laminack, L., & Kelly, K. (2019). *Reading to make a difference: Using literature to help students speak freely, think deeply, and take action*. Portsmouth, NH: Heinemann.

Lancia, P. J. (1997). Literary borrowing: The effects of literature on children's writing. *The Reading Teacher, 50*(6), 470–475.

Lannin, A. (2014). The sound of pencils on the page: Freewriting in a junior high school classroom. *Writing and Pedagogy, 6*(3), 555–581.

Lee, E. & Alvarez, S. P. (2020). World Englishes, translingualism, and racialization in the US college composition classroom. *World Englishes, 39*(2), 263–274.

Lee & Low Books, Jiménez, L. M., & Beckert, B. (2020, January 28). Where is the diversity in publishing? The 2019 diversity baseline survey results. Lee & Low Blog.

Lehner-Quam, A., West, R., & Espinosa, C. (forthcoming). Developing and teaching with a diverse children's literature collection at an urban public college: What teacher education students know and ways their knowledge can grow about diverse books. *Behavioral & Social Sciences Librarian Journal*.

Lewison, M., Leland, C., & Harste, J. (2014) *Creating critical classrooms: Reading and writing with an edge* (2nd edition). New York: Routledge.

López-Robertson, J. (2017). Diciendo cuentos/Telling stories: Learning from and about the community cultural wealth of Latina mamás through Latino children's literature. *Language Arts, 95*(1), 7–16.

Mahoney, K. (2017). *The assessment of emergent bilinguals: Supporting English language learners.* Clevedon, UK: Multilingual Matters.

Martínez-Álvarez, P. (2019). Dis/ability labels and emergent bilingual children: Current research and new possibilities to grow as bilingual and biliterate learners. *Ethnicity and Education,* 174–193.

Martínez-Roldán, C. M. (2005). The inquiry acts of bilingual children in literature discussions. *Language Arts, 83*(1), 22–32.

Menken, K., Pérez Rosario, V., & Guzmán Valerio, L. A. (2018). Increasing multilingualism in schoolscapes: New scenery and language education policies. *Linguistic Landscape, 4*(2), 101–127.

Mercado, C. (2005). Seeing what's there: Language and literacy funds of knowledge in New York Puerto Rican homes. In A. C. Zentella (Ed.) *Building on strength: Language and literacy in Latino families and communities.* New York: Teachers College Columbia University Press.

Minor, C. (2019). *We got this: Equity, access, and the quest to be who our students need us to be.* Portsmouth, NH: Heinemann.

Moll, L. C., Amanti, C., Neff, D., & Gonzalez, N. (1992). Funds of knowledge for teaching: Using a qualitative approach to connect homes and classrooms. *Theory Into Practice, 31*(2), 132–141.

Moll, L. C., Sáez, R., & Dworin, J. (2001). Exploring biliteracy: Two student case examples of writing as a social practice. *Elementary School Journal, 101*(4).

National Institute of Child Health & Human Development (2000). Report of the National Reading Panel. *Teaching children to read: An evidence-based assessment of the scientific research literature on reading and its implication for reading instruction.* (NIH Publication No. 00-4769). Washington, DC: U.S. Government Printing Office.

Osorio, S. L. (2020). Building culturally and linguistically sustaining spaces for emergent bilinguals: Using read-alouds to promote translanguaging. *The Reading Teacher.*

Pérez Rosario, V. (2015). *Translanguaging in Latino/a literature: A guide for educators.* New York: The CUNY-NYSIEB.

Peterson, R., & Eeds, M. (2007). *Grand conversations: Literature groups in action.* New York: Scholastic.

Pratt, M. L. (1991). Arts of the contact zone. *Profession,* 33–40. Retrieved June 5, 2020, from jstor.org/stable/25595469

Read, C. (1986). *Children's creative spelling.* London: Routledge & Kegan Paul.

Rosa, J., & Flores, N. (2017). Unsettling race and language: Toward a raciolinguistic perspective. *Language in Society, 46*(5), 621–647. doi:10.1017/S0047404517000562

Rosenblatt, L. M. (1978). *The reader, the text, the poem: The transactional theory of the literary work.* Carbondale, IL: Southern Illinois University Press.

Rosenblatt, L. M. (1995). *Literature as exploration* (5th edition). The Modern Language Association of America.

Roth, K., & Dabrowski, J. (2016). *Interactive writing across grades: A small practice with big results.* Portsmouth, NH: Stenhouse.

Routman, R. (2005). *Writing essentials.* Portsmouth, NH: Heinemann.

Samway, K. (2006). *When English language learners write: Connecting research to practice, K–8.* Portsmouth, NH: Heinemann.

Scharer, P. (2016). *Responsive literacy: A comprehensive framework.* New York: Scholastic.

Serna, I., & Hudelson, S. (1993). Becoming a writer of Spanish and English. *Quarterly of the National Writing Project and the Center for the Study of Writing and Literacy, 15*(1), 1–5.

Shanahan, T. (October 20, 2020). Letters in phonemic awareness instruction or the reciprocal nature of learning to read. Shanahan on Literacy.

Sims Bishop, R. (1990). Mirrors, windows, and sliding glass doors. *Perspectives: Choosing and using books for the classroom, 6*(3).

Smith, F. (1983). Reading like a writer. *Language Arts, 60*(5), 558–567.

Smith, K. (1995). Bringing children and literature together in the elementary classroom. *Primary Voices, 3*(2), 22–32.

Stead, T. (2001). *Is that a fact? Teaching non-fiction, K–3.* Portsmouth, NH: Stenhouse Publishers.

Stephens, D., Harste, J., & Clyde, J. A. (2019). *Reading revealed: 50 expert teachers share what they do and why they do it.* New York: Scholastic.

Strieb, L., with Carini, P., Kanevsky, R., & Wice, B. (2011). *Prospects descriptive processes: The child, the art of teaching, and the classroom and school, revised edition.* The Prospect Archives and Center for Education and Research, North Bennington, VT.

Sugarman, J., & Geary, C. (2018). English learners in select States: Demographics, outcomes, and state accountability policies. Washington, DC: Migration Policy Institute.

Taberski, S. (2000). *On solid ground: Strategies for teaching reading, K–3.* Portsmouth, NH: Heinemann.

Taberski, S. (2010). *Comprehension from the ground up: Simplified, sensible instruction for the K–3 reading workshop.* Portsmouth, NH: Heinemann.

Velasco, P., & García, O. (2014). Translanguaging and the writing of bilingual learners. *Bilingual Research Journal, 37*(1), 6–23.

Velasco, P. & Espinosa, C. (forthcoming). *An introduction to classroom practices for multilingual learners/English language learners and the next generation English language arts learning standards.* Office of Bilingual Education and World Languages. New York State Education Department.

Vogel, S., Hoadley, C., Ascenzi-Moreno, L., & Menken, K. (2019). The role of translanguaging in computational literacies: Documenting middle school bilinguals' practices in computer science integrated units. Proceedings of the 50th ACM Technical Symposium on Computer Science Education, 1164–1170.

Vogel, S. (2020). *Translanguaging about, with, and through code and computing: Emergent bi/multilingual middle schoolers forging computational literacies.* Unpublished Dissertation. The Graduate Center of the City University of New York.

Vygotsky, L. S. (1978). *Mind in society: The development of higher psychological processes.* Cambridge, UK: Harvard University Press.

Wang, Y., & Zheng, Y. (2014). "Drive my mind into thinking": Using freewriting In an English language learning classroom. *Talking Points, 26*(1), 11–18.

Wei, L. (2011). Moment analysis and translanguaging space: Discursive constructions of identities by multilingual Chinese youth in Britain. *Journal of Pragmatics, 43,* 1222–1235.

Wells, G. (1985). The meaning makers: *Children learning language and using language to learn.* Portsmouth, NH: Heinemann.

Wells, G. (2009). *The meaning makers: Learning to talk and talking to learn* (2nd edition). Multilingual Matters.

Wessels, S., & Herrera, S. (2013). Drawing their way into writing: Culturally and linguistically diverse students finding voice through mini-novelas. *TESOL Journal, 5*(1), 105–119.

Westover, T. (2018). *Educated: A memoir.* New York: Random House.

Whitmore, K. (2015). Becoming the story in the joyful world of "Jack and the Beanstalk." *Language Arts, 93*(1), 25–37.

Wilde, S. (2000). *Miscue analysis made easy: Building on student strengths.* Portsmouth, NH: Heinemann.

Wood Ray, K. (1999). *Wondrous words: Writers and writing in the elementary classroom.* Urbana, IL: National Council of Teachers of English.

Wood Ray, K. (2010). *In pictures and in words: Teaching the qualities of good writing through illustration study.* Portsmouth, NH: Heinemann.

Wood Ray, K., & Cleaveland, L. (2018). *A teacher's guide to getting started with beginning writers: The classroom essentials series.* Portsmouth, NH: Heinemann.

Wood Ray, K., & Glover, M. (2008). *Already ready: Nurturing writers in preschool and kindergarten.* Portsmouth, NH: Heinemann.

Wood Ray, K., & Laminack, L. (2001). *The writing workshop: Working through the hard parts (and they're all hard parts).* Portsmouth, NH: Heinemann.

Zapata, A., & Laman, T. (2016). "I write to show how beautiful my languages are": Translingual writing instruction in English-dominant classrooms. *Language Arts, 93*(5), 366–378.

INDEX